Table of Contents

Publisher's Preface
iii

Foreword
v

Acknowledgments
vii

Dedication
ix

Introduction
1

Chapter 1
Historical, Anthropological, and Religious
Characteristics in Cambodia
5

Chapter 2
An Analysis of the History of the Assemblies of God
and Cultural Dynamics in Cambodia
25

Chapter 3
An Analysis of the Missions Practices Used
and Projections for the Future
49

Bibliography
77

Appendices
83

Joshua J. Lovelace

FROM SEEDTIME
to *Harvest*

The History of
the Assemblies of God
in Cambodia

WIPF & STOCK · Eugene, Oregon

Pentecost Around the World Book 5

Foreword by Edward L. Smither

Wipf and Stock Publishers
199 W 8th Ave, Suite 3
Eugene, OR 97401

From Seedtime To Harvest
The History of the Assemblies of God in Cambodia
By Lovelace, Joshua J. and Smither, Edward L.
Copyright © 2019 APTS Press All rights reserved.
Softcover ISBN-13: 978-1-5326-9216-1
Hardcover ISBN-13: 978-1-5326-9217-8
eBook ISBN-13: 978-1-5326-9218-5
Publication date 5/20/2019
Previously published by APTS Press, 2019

Publisher's Preface

to the *Pentecost Around the World* Book Series

We are pleased to announce that this new book, *From Seedtime to Harvest: The History of the Assemblies of God in Cambodia*, is the fifth volume in our Pentecost Around the World series. The purpose of this series is to provide a place for historical reflection on what God is doing through the Pentecostal Movement, particularly in the Asia Pacific and Pacific Oceana regions of the world.

The four previous titles are, *Reflections of an Early American Pentecostal*, by Stanley Horton, *The Cross Among Pagodas: A History of the Assemblies of God in Myanmar* by Chin Khua Khai, *Pentecost to the Uttermost: A History of the Assemblies of God in Samoa* and *Pentecostal Pioneer: The Life and Legacy of Rudy Esperanza and the Early Years of the Assemblies of God in the Philippines* by Dynnice Rosanny D. Engcoy.

Unfortunately, the first three books are no longer available. Dynnice Engcoy's book is available for purchase through our website, www.aptspress.org.

If you have any questions or comments, you are welcome to contact us through our website.

We hope you enjoy this book.

The PUBLISHER

Foreword

The prominent church historian Justo Gonzalez once asserted that the history of the church is the history of mission. More than the history of buildings, doctrines, or famous theologians, church history is a narrative of God's mission among all peoples. Recognizing how the gospel has spread into different parts of the world and to different cultures, it is an uneven, messy, but amazing story.

While we look forward in mission and strive to develop strategies for reaching a rapidly changing world with the gospel, we must also look back. How were churches planted? Who were the missionaries? What were their strategies? What mistakes did they make? What innovative approaches did they take? What do these voices teach us for mission today? To look back and reflect is an exercise in humility. It means that we actually have something to learn from the past. It first means that we accurately understand the past—the good, the bad, and the ugly. It is an honest inquiry. When we've humbly engaged in the study of mission history, we realize that this is ultimately God's work and we get to participate in it.

In this work, Josh Lovelace invites us to grasp the story of the Assemblies of God mission in Cambodia, which began in the late twentieth century. The decades of war and even genocide in the southeast Asian nation seemed to prompt a greater openness to the gospel message. Assemblies of God missionaries responded to the call and have faithfully served the peoples of Cambodia in evangelism, church planting, and other aspects of Christian mission over the past few decades. As we meet the growing church in Cambodia, let us learn from the Assemblies of God mission journey, and reflect on how we ought to move forward in twenty-first century mission. In the end, let us pause and give thanks to God for his faithfulness to bless all peoples (Gen 12:3).

Edward L. Smither, PhD
Dean, College of Intercultural Studies
Columbia International University

Acknowledgments

This work was birthed from a desire to know more about the initial history of the Assemblies of God in Cambodia. Various missionaries and pastors had stories to share and each made significant contributions of their time and expertise. It is a privilege to serve with these wonderful individuals who continually demonstrate a call to serve among the Khmer people.

I am indebted to many people who are part of the ministries at Asia Pacific Theological Seminary in Baguio City, Philippines. Dave Johnson does a tremendous job serving as the director for APTS Press. I appreciate his enthusiasm to provide resources which assist our fellow brothers and sisters throughout Asia. Sam Bowdoin has served in various capacities at APTS and currently serves as the director for ICI Philippines. He was an amazing thesis mentor and provided continual insight throughout the research and writing process. Moreover, APTS Press editors Frank McNelis, Jon Smith and Joy Varnell assisted in countless ways to make the manuscript even more readable. Thank you for lending your skills to this project.

My family (Carmen, Emma, and Jude) have always been my biggest cheerleaders and give encouragement when I need it most. They are a wonderful team as we serve together in Cambodia. Thank you for your love and willingness in all areas.

Above all, praise and honor to Jesus Christ for His strength throughout this project. He is Lord of the harvest in Cambodia.

Dedication

This work is dedicated to
the persevering Khmer church leaders
and pioneer missionaries of the 1990s.
Christianity has advanced
in Cambodia because of you.

Introduction

His name was Vith. Our paths first crossed in April 2012 when I went to his small store to purchase 20-liter water bottles for our family's supply of drinking water. His smile was pleasant, his eyes twinkled, and he was always eager to demonstrate quality service. Normally, Vith was already running toward me before I could park my Toyota Hilux truck and then he would linger afterwards to converse about various topics. Time after time the routine was the same—stopping at his store to purchase drinking water followed by pleasant conversation.

October 23, 2012, was a different day at the water store, however, which ultimately changed my life and perspective. For that particular day allowed me to see a different side of Vith and a different side of life in Cambodia. I did not immediately see my friend but waited for several minutes in the small, dusty parking area in front of his store. Instead of running to greet me, he slowly emerged from under the tattered green awning that draped across the entryway. His feet slowly kicked the dust while his eyes were firmly fixed upon the ground, as if he didn't want to make eye contact with me. The wide-open smile, abundant kindness, carefree attitude, and prompt service were all missing. Time seemed to stand still as I waited for him to approach my truck.

Sticking my head out the window, I greeted Vith in the Khmer language then asked how he was doing. The short distance he traversed usually took a few seconds, but that day it seemed to take minutes as he eventually arrived at the side of my truck, all the while keeping his eyes pointed downward. I gently spoke again and patiently waited for his response, sensing that something was definitely wrong. He finally made eye contact with me as he spoke words that yet ring in my ears and I feel in my inmost being. He quietly yet firmly stated, "I have no hope in this life."

Over the next few minutes, Vith described situation after situation and problem after problem, all the while repeating the same phrase in Khmer: "I have no hope. I have no hope. I have no hope." It was at that moment I realized two distinct actualities. First, the Lord had provided an opportunity to share the message of hope in Jesus Christ with an individual; and second, I was cut to pieces with the reality that's common to so many who live in Cambodia. The records of history I had previously read about civil war, genocide, displacement, border camps, and rebuilding a country, etc., flashed before my eyes in those few moments in that small, dusty parking lot in Siem Reap Province. It was painfully evident that life can be without hope, and many in Cambodia face this actuality each day.

This incident continually reminds me of the reason for cross-cultural ministry in places such as Cambodia. It is for people like Vith that missionaries leave their home country to adopt a new country of residence, learn a new language which they speak from their head instead of their heart. It is for people like Vith missionaries search for ways to minister, in a contextualized manner, in order to convey the message of hope in Jesus Christ. Moreover, it is because of this situation, which can be observed worldwide, that the Assemblies of God has been vigilant for the past century to ensure that missionaries are sent to foreign lands to reach the lost, plant churches, train believers, and serve with compassion. This was the scenario in 1990 when the Assemblies of God entered Cambodia and started working with believers to establish a national church known as the Assemblies of God Cambodia (AGC).

Although our Fellowship has maintained a presence in Cambodia since 1990, little has ever been recorded about the Assemblies of God Cambodia by means of in-depth research and writing. It appears that many individuals (both Khmer pastors and expatriate missionaries) carry noteworthy components regarding the history of the Assemblies of God in Cambodia. However, the majority of those individuals have not had an opportunity to contribute to the telling of various historical events. It is this particular notion that has helped me recognize the need to resource our Fellowship, and other ministry networks, in regard to our history and its significance.

Students of history, specifically church history, are always intrigued by the concept of collecting data that can serve to make past events come alive. Furthermore, this endeavor encompasses the chronological framework of the past, present, and future to demonstrate how a movement came into existence, explain its current functions and purposes, as well as provide an indicator for the days to come. These aspects related to time (especially the significance of past events) have brought me to a place of continually searching to understand the how's and why's of the present time as we examine the past and speed toward new opportunities on distant horizons.

Since my arrival in Cambodia in 2010, I have sought to find any attainable annals or other sources of history related to the Assemblies of God and its ministry among the Khmer people in Cambodia. This opportunity has enabled me to survey the detailed historical context through a three-fold lens: a historical background of the Khmer people, an analysis of the Assemblies of God's 25 years in Cambodia (1990-2015), and a proposed application that can provide foresight into the next 25 years. These foundational areas of Khmer history, events within the Assemblies of God in Cambodia, and analysis of how the past could shape the future will demonstrate the significance of the past two-and-a-half decades both inside and outside the realm of Christianity.

The primary research involved with this project is three-fold: historical literature, anthropological application, and personal interviews. In regard to history, various sources have been tapped to provide an overview of Cambodia's recent history, including the key turning points; this takes into account the overall relation to the Khmer people, religious trends, and society in general. Anthropological aspects are taken into account via various assessments that are connected to historical characteristics and provide a detailed analysis to shed light on the intricacies of culture and worldview. Lastly, personal interviews with Assemblies of God pastors, leaders, and missionaries function as a means to illustrate events and details, along with notable trends and patterns, which shaped the Fellowship from 1990 to 2015. This specific approach to research then allows the writer to make a proposal, as those involved with the Assemblies of God look ahead to the next 25 years.

Chapter 1

Historical, Anthropological, and Religious Characteristics in Cambodia

History and Religion of the Khmer People

The Khmer people of Cambodia (also known as Kampuchea) have a rich history that spans thousands of years in Southeast Asia. Within the earliest Khmer kingdoms, there was a continual emphasis on agricultural improvements, creation and maintenance of ranks within society, and intense reverence related to religious practices.[1] Special bonds linked the earliest rulers and their subjects within a framework of Indian ideologies, which enabled participation in society and the worship of Hindu deities. These early years of history continued to develop into a structured system of patrons and clients, while the overall emphasis of the community was viewed in a collective sense.[2]

From the establishment of the Khmer Empire in the early 9th century until its demise in the 15th century, the authoritarian leader of the people was seen as its most vital facet. This period of history clearly demonstrated that a king kept the empire from collapsing and was thought to possess supernatural powers in order to maintain stability.[3] Although he was viewed on a much

---

[1] David P. Chandler, *The Land and People of Cambodia* (New York, NY: HarperCollins Publishers, 1991), 44.

[2] Ibid., 19.

[3] Ibid., 59.

higher level than the common Khmer, there was a unique bond between king and people. Patronage and mutual responsibilities extended from the extravagant palace to the lowest rice paddy and allocated a viable network within the empire.[4] This connection brought security from top to bottom, since it was repeated by each succeeding king. Precedents were instituted in this way by the earliest kings at Angkor to ensure continuance of the empire and to sustain an effective administration.

As kings literally made their mark in history with buildings and temples dedicated to Hindu deities or members of the royal family, Buddhism began growing and was recognized on a larger scale. A new structure of merit through Buddhism was introduced to redeem the kingdom from previous conquerors and enabled new construction efforts at Angkor, with special attention given to the Buddha.[5] Since the period of significant transformation, Theravada Buddhism has dictated Khmer practices, traditions, and ideologies for the past 800 years, with the only break in this religious dominance occurring during the Khmer Rouge regime.

Early Catholic and Protestant Missions

Christianity was introduced to Cambodia through the work of Catholic missionaries in the 16th century, as the Dominicans (also known as the Order of the Preachers) received their commission to serve during the age of exploration. While some Christian communities in Southeast Asia were unable to maintain longevity, various areas near modern-day Cambodia experienced permanence.[6] Among the Dominicans sent from

---

[4]David P. Chandler, *A History of Cambodia*, 2nd ed. (Chiang Mai, Thailand: Silkworm Books, 1998), 48.

[5]Ibid., 58.

[6]Samuel H. Moffett, *A History of Christianity in Asia Vol. 2 1500-1900*, (Maryknoll, NY: Orbis Books, 2005), 37.

Portugal was Gaspar da Cruz, who had the opportunity to travel to what is modern-day India, Sri Lanka, and Malaysia. He departed from the Portuguese colony of Malacca in 1555 to sail across the Gulf of Thailand and travel three months upstream along the Mekong River.[7] In doing so, he was the first missionary to serve among the Khmer.

Protestants in Cambodia first arrived in the early part of the 17th century via Dutch traders and merchants. As trading relationships progressed with the Khmer in 1601, missionary work became a definite possibility.[8] The Dutch quickly seized upon this opportunity to obtain greater influence in Southeast Asia, while various other countries were jockeying for power and control. Unfortunately, their approach was quite different from the other European nations of that particular era, which would lead to future challenges. Spain and Portugal, for example, desired profit but always maintained a passion for evangelism; whereas the Dutch were merely motivated by commerce to the point of hiring clergymen who showed greater interest in business than in preaching the gospel.[9] Overall, the first Protestants continually struggled due to their divided interests in the midst of opportunities to minister among the Khmer.

Christianity in Cambodia between the 16th and the 19th centuries was truly challenging. There were numerous martyrs and very few conversions during the 300 years from Gaspar de Cruz's missions work in 1555 until the protectorate under France, which was formed in 1863.[10] Estimates (for both Protestants and Catholics) in Cambodia of conversions are

---

[7]De Castro, Joaquim Magalhães. "Great Figures of the Missionary Work," www.oclarim.com.mo/en/2016/07/01/gaspar-da-cruz-the-dominican-traveller-5 (accessed on August 18, 2016).

[8]Edward Heawood, *A History of Geographical Discovery in the Seventeenth and Eighteenth Centuries* (New York, NY: Cambridge University Press, 2012), 86.

[9]Samuel H. Moffett, *A History of Christianity in Asia Vol. 2: 1500-1900*, 214.

[10]Ibid., 25.

merely in the hundreds by the time the French established their presence in Indochina. Furthermore, many of the Christians at that time were comprised of other nationalities, including Chinese, Vietnamese, and French, with an extremely small number being Khmer.[11] As for missionary activities at the hands of the Protestants, the work had been quite regular and visible among the Khmer for over 200 years, yet a long-term presence remained elusive. Some estimates show there were approximately 600 Catholic adherents but the number of Protestants remains unknown.[12]

The French Protectorate, which controlled Cambodia from 1863 to 1953, offered little assistance in regard to Christianity. France's presence in Cambodia was primarily political, as their leaders endeavored to maintain colonial influence throughout Southeast Asia. While additional Catholic missionaries were sent to Cambodia, Protestants were prohibited from missions' activity during the initial decades of French rule.[13] Overall, this caused the Khmer to view Christianity as a foreign entity that was simply attached to political motives.

Christianity in the Early 20th Century

The turning point for Christianity in Cambodia came 60 years after creation of the French Protectorate, as Protestants were able to start the first long-term missions' work among the Khmer. The arrival of two families in 1923 serving with the Christian and Missionary Alliance (CMA) was truly monumental, yet there was little fanfare to mark the occasion.

---

[11]Saiyasak, Chansamone. "Southeast Asia Christianity," www.academia.edu/4781739/Southeast_Asia_Christianity (accessed on August 12, 2016).

[12]Steven J. Hyde, "A Missiological and Critical Study of Cambodia's Historical, Cultural, and Sociopolitical Characteristics to Identify the Factors of Rapid Church Growth and Propose Its Future Prognosis" (PhD diss, Bethany International University, 2015), 25.

[13]Ibid., 24.

The families—Mr. and Mrs. Arthur Hammond and Mr. and Mrs. David Ellison—were welcomed by a French official who boldly declared their work would not have any success in Cambodia.[14] Undaunted, the Hammonds and Ellisons forged ahead to create ministry sites with the intention of long-duration activity among the Khmer.

The Hammonds were situated in Phnom Penh and focused on translating the Bible into the Khmer language, while the Ellisons moved to northwest Cambodia to start a center for training pastors and evangelists.[15] During the subsequent decades, just as with their missionary predecessors, there were many challenges in addition to waves of persecution. However, a long-term missionary base allowed for effective ministry among the Khmer, with a focus on providing the Scriptures in their own language and on training leaders to adequately convey the message of Christ. In 30 years, the Bible was completely translated into the Khmer language, a seminary was in operation, and house churches were planted in various parts of the country.[16]

From the changing winds of politics in Asia, radical Communist ideologies continued to spread. However, despite the small number of believers in places like Cambodia, Christianity advanced.[17] Cambodia was no stranger to instability due to Communism. This was the primary impetus within politics and played a significant role in evangelism because the number of Christians continued to increase. Unfortunately, that growth was short-lived when the greatest persecution in Cambodia occurred from 1975 to 1979. As Steven Cormack states regarding those years, "To be a Christian in

---

[14]Don Cormack, *Killing Field, Living Fields* (London, UK: Monarch Books, 2001), 57.
[15]Ibid., 57.
[16]Ibid., 64.
[17]Stephen Neill, *A History of Christian Missions* (London, UK: Penguin Books, 1991), 476.

Cambodian society was to be a social pariah, misunderstood and ill-treated, a convenient scapegoat for blame and abuse."[18] This reality was taken to a heightened level during the three and a half years of genocide, as nearly all 10,000 Christians in Cambodia were eliminated.[19]

Year Zero: The Magnitude of the Khmer Rouge

Civil War and Genocide

"To keep you is no benefit and to kill you is no loss." These words were recognized as a callous anthem from the lips of the Khmer Rouge cadres as they demonstrated the most vicious behavior throughout Cambodia. Although estimates vary regarding the loss of life, a common consensus shows that approximately two million Khmer perished by the means of execution, disease, and starvation. Fathers, mothers, brothers, sisters, fellow co-workers, common citizens—all were affected, none being immune to this reign of terror. It has been widely noted among the Khmer that every family experienced the loss of loved ones, with some families being entirely eradicated. The reality of this tragedy is that the suffering did not come by the hands of foreigners but from their own countrymen.

Although the genocide started in 1975, the chaos of civil war engulfed Cambodia eight years prior to the fall of Phnom Penh. The early months of 1967 were filled with political clashes, rebellions led by enthusiastic vigilantes, and public executions as various groups jostled for power.[20] In addition to these factions,

---

[18]Don Cormack, *Killing Fields, Living Fields,* 64.

[19]Steven J. Hyde, "A Missiological and Critical Study of Cambodia's Historical, Cultural, and Sociopolitical Characteristics to Identify the Factors of Rapid Church Growth and Propose its Future Prognosis," 47.

[20]David P. Chandler, *The Tragedy of Cambodian History* (Chiang Mai, Thailand: Silkworm Books, 1993), 165.

the Vietnamese War had spilled across the border into the eastern provinces of Cambodia, which brought American involvement to a heightened level among the Khmer politicians and would-be leaders.

The breaking point came in 1970, when Prince Norodom Sihanouk was forced out of power via a coup that placed Lon Nol in power, with the backing of American support. For many of the Khmer in the early 1970s, the chaos was choking the country, yet they looked to their new leader with Western resources as a suitable patron to ensure survival. Lon Nol himself demonstrated a certain invincibility, which was derived from the previous glories of the Khmer Empire coupled with blessings from Buddhist monks.[21] The success of the new government and the trust of the people lasted only five years, as the Khmer Rouge swept through the countryside with plans for radical change.

Cambodia's "day of infamy," April 17, 1975, arrived with fanfare mixed with great suspicion. At that time, Phnom Penh was flooded with refugees looking for temporary safety in the capital city due to the intense conflict in the provincial areas. They longed for liberation from the civil war, but the frequent changes of power from the previous years left many uncertain on that particular April morning. The black-clad army's slow procession down the major avenues eventually turned into two million people being pushed into the countryside to await an uncertain fate.[22]

Beginning with the centuries of splendor at Angkor until the centuries of suppression from neighboring countries, the Khmer always found a way to forge ahead by aligning themselves in the most advantageous way with various individuals of influence. However, from April 1975 until January 1979, the only

---

[21]Ibid., 205.
[22]David P. Chandler, *A History of Cambodia*, 2nd ed, 208.

compatriots for the Khmer were suffering and death through the actions of their extreme Communist overseers. Overall, the intention of making a "Year Zero" by returning to a total agrarian society was complete, as nearly 2,000 years of history and tradition were replaced with radical, revolutionary objectives.

Labor camps were built throughout the country, with city dwellers and rural farmers alike conformed into what the Khmer Rouge viewed as a countryside utopia consisting of planting rice and digging irrigation ditches. At the same time, Christians, Buddhist monks, Muslims, Vietnamese, and other minorities were intentionally separated and eliminated. The days were filled with grueling work, while the evenings included indoctrination classes in order to keep everyone in line with *Angkar*: the Khmer word meaning "the organization" (a.k.a., the new authority in Cambodia).[23] Coupled with the physical and emotional struggles was the constant fear of being summoned by the *Angkar* for various offenses. This dreadful "call" led many Khmer to places such as S-21, a notorious prison in Phnom Penh previously used as a high school. It was there that as many as 20,000 people were tortured, interrogated, and killed, with only six survivors remaining after three and a half years.[24]

Vietnamese Occupation

The Vietnamese invasion in December 1978 led to the liberation of Phnom Penh on January 7, 1979. The Khmer Rouge fled to the jungles in western Cambodia, as the country was left in shambles with millions dead and millions more displaced and in disarray. A nation previously renowned for peace, gentleness, and civility was unrecognizable due to the carnage of war and

---

[23]David P. Chandler, *The Tragedy of Cambodian History*, 260.
[24]Ibid., 285.

genocide against its own people. As for the Christians at the time of Vietnamese "liberation" in 1979, it is estimated the survivors numbered about 150. Nearly all pastors were eliminated, leaving the remaining believers without any type of leadership. The words of the Khmer Rouge cadres— "Blood makes the ground softer"—demonstrate the brutality of their regime as well as the repetition of persecution against Christianity in Cambodia.[25]

Displacement abounded as refugee camps were created along the Thailand-Cambodia border. Matters were made worse as famine became widespread in 1979-1980 due to the abandonment of fields, which ultimately led to vast numbers who suffered from starvation.[26] The refugee camps filled with the dying and the bones of the fallen still scattered along roads and trails were grim reminders of the prior years.

In the midst of this madness, Christianity grew by the thousands among the refugees in the border camps, with new churches holding worship services.[27] However, the Vietnamese demonstrated no tolerance toward the Christians and the proclamation of the gospel. Thus, life under the Vietnam occupation was only slightly better than that under the Khmer Rouge, as the new captors oppressed the Khmer people and targeted Christians with vicious persecution.[28]

September 1989 marked the end of Vietnamese control in Cambodia after maintaining "order" for ten years. Although the Khmer were in the process of trying to rebuild all aspects of life and society, the hope of re-establishing a country of their own

---

[25]Steven J. Hyde, "A Missiological and Critical Study of Cambodia's Historical, Cultural, and Sociopolitical Characteristics to Identify the Factors of Rapid Church Growth and Propose its Future Prognosis," 25.

[26]David P. Chandler, *The Land and People of Cambodia*, 159.

[27]Don Cormack, *Killing Fields, Living Fields*, 334.

[28]Steven J. Hyde, "A Missiological and Critical Study of Cambodia's Historical, Cultural, and Sociopolitical Characteristics to Identify the Factors of Rapid Church Growth and Propose its Future Prognosis," 57.

seemed distant at best. The border camps were closed in the early 1990s; and repatriation was widespread for the survivors of civil war, genocide, and forced occupation. In addition, Christian growth among the refugees ended as thousands joined a worldwide dispersion to begin a new life abroad.[29] The estimate of 150 believers in 1979, which had grown to several thousand in the camps in the 1980s, fell back to only 200 by the time the Vietnamese left in 1989. It seemed Christianity in Cambodia had to start over; however, no one could have ever imagined the changes that were to occur in the 1990s.

The Assemblies of God in Cambodia

An Open Door Via Unconventional Methods

"Long live the Assemblies of God!" These are words that were never expected to be heard from the mouth of a Communist official in Cambodia, especially while religious activity was prohibited. However, this is how God opened the doors to Assemblies of God (AG) missionaries in 1990.

As the Vietnamese were in the process of leaving Cambodia in 1989, the AG strategized to enter the country and minister to the Khmer. Missionary Ron Maddux (the AG's area director for Peninsular Asia from 1990 to 1998) was overseeing the missions work within Cambodia, Vietnam, Laos, and Myanmar. Based in Bangkok, Thailand, he made plans to visit Cambodia after the Vietnamese occupation. Through a process of meetings regarding protocols and visas, Maddux traveled to Laos, which was one of the few countries in Asia that had a Cambodian embassy. He simply explained to the embassy officials that his purpose for going to Cambodia was to provide assistance to the many needs of the Khmer. The officials could not understand

---

[29]Don Cormack, *Killing Fields, Living Fields,* 341.

why anyone would want to go to Cambodia because of the continued violence, but they acquiesced and gave permission for a single trip.

In March 1990, Maddux made that trip, along with missionary Bob Houlihan, who was the AG regional director for the Asia Pacific region. Once there, they obtained an appointment at the Ministry of Foreign Affairs, hoping to connect with the right people and receive permission for Assemblies of God missionaries to serve long-term in Cambodia. As they spoke to the officials, Maddux took a Sharp Wizard memo-taker out of his pocket to record details as Houlihan continued to explain the intentions of their trip. An office staff person, noticing the device, asked Maddux if he was a computer expert. Before he could answer for himself, Houlihan exclaimed, "Yes, he's a computer whiz."

The two missionaries were almost immediately ushered into another room where there was a computer that appeared to be inoperable; and Maddux was asked if he could fix it since he was previously noted as being an "expert." Quietly praying to himself, he nervously worked at the desk while surrounded by government officials and hard-nosed Communists, who closely watched his every move. After trying various procedures to reboot the computer, he finally got it up and running. It was at that moment a Cambodian official named Heng Samok gleefully shouted, "Long live the Assemblies of God!"

Heng Samok took time to meet with Houlihan and Maddux and asked how he could help them in their endeavors to get AG personnel into the country. The result was the granting of five visas for Ron to make five separate trips to visit Phnom Penh and plan for future missionary activities among the Khmer people. Overjoyed with the repaired computer, a Communist official allowed Christian workers into this war-torn, devastated country that had countless needs.

(Many years later, Maddux was preaching at the International Christian Assembly in Cambodia and shared with the congregation about that event in 1990, stating, "No one could ever plan that. No one could ever strategize that. God uses unconventional methods."[30] For it was the first time these government officials had ever heard about the Assemblies of God and, of course, their Communist mindset caused them to have no sympathy toward Christian ministries. However, God was working and opened the door to new possibilities in Cambodia.)

The Dorsey Family

Upon returning to Bangkok, Maddux met with the AG missionaries in Thailand to share about his and Houlihan's meeting as well as the future possibilities. Then they all prayed for God to stir up a desire in the hearts of missionaries to serve among the Khmer. Every few months, Maddux would make another trip from Bangkok to Phnom Penh (via Vientiane) to explore possibilities and to survey the scenario in Cambodia. With the missionaries in Thailand continuing to pray, one family—Randy and Carolyn Dorsey, along with their two daughters—believed that God was calling them to transition from Thailand to Cambodia.

The Dorseys arrived June 1990 in Phnom Penh to serve as the first resident AG missionaries in Cambodia. Under various guidelines with the Cambodian government, they were permitted to establish children's homes and medical clinics in addition to teaching English as a second language.[31] Since

---

[30]Ron Maddux, "The Assemblies of God in Cambodia" (International Christian Assembly, Phnom Penh, Cambodia, January 27, 2016).

[31]Carolyn Dorsey, "Information Regarding the Founding of the Assemblies of God Work in Cambodia" (Paper Presented for the Assemblies of God Missionary Fellowship, May, 2005).

Christianity was prohibited by the government, these areas of ministry were to be the major focus for the AG. However, another ministry for the Dorseys was about to happen "by accident" in September 1990—establishment of the International Christian Assembly.[32]

The International Christian Assembly

Just as many great endeavors originate from small beginnings, this was the situation as the Dorsey family met with other missions' workers on Sunday mornings. The gatherings started at the Hotel Asie on Monivong Boulevard and were later moved to 102 Toul Samuth Boulevard near the Independence Monument, which provided a place not only to worship, but also for the AG field office.[33] Casual times of devotions, fellowship, prayer, and worship took shape as the informal group developed into a church with more and more people joining in attendance.

Due to its continued growth, which included various nationalities, the ICA changed locations three more times in the 1990s in order to keep pace with its increasing congregation and ongoing ministries. It met in the auditorium at the International School of Phnom Penh from 1992 to 1997, then met in the auditorium at the World Vision office from 1997 to 2011.[34] Still needing a larger campus, the church partnered with the Assemblies of God Missionary Fellowship (AGMF) and the Cambodia Bible Institute (CBI) to build a facility at its current location—37M Street 16 in Teuk Thla Commune. Today, the ICA has ministries for adults, youth, and children representing

---

[32]Carolyn Dorsey, "History of ICA Phnom Penh" (Paper presented for the Assemblies of God Missionary Fellowship, February, 2000).
   [33]Ibid.
   [34]Ibid.

over 30 nationalities, with a regular Sunday attendance of over 400.[35]

Jerusalem Church and Pastor Heng Cheng

When the Dorsey family moved to Cambodia, Jerusalem Church in Phnom Penh already had a very significant role among the Khmer. Started in 1985, it ministered to people in the midst of rebuilding after the civil war, genocide at the hands of the Khmer Rouge, and a decade of Vietnamese occupation. Pastor Heng Cheng, who provided leadership within the ministries at Jerusalem Church, played an integral role in the future of Christianity among the Khmer. Furthermore, the church had the distinction of becoming the first Assemblies of God church in Cambodia.

Heng Cheng was born in Kampot Province in 1947 to a Christian family. He relocated to Phnom Penh in the early 1970s to serve as a captain in the Khmer Republic military and to study at the Faculty of Medicine. Shortly after the Khmer Rouge took control of Phnom Penh in April 1975, Cheng fled to Vietnam. He spent the next three and a half years there and was one of the few former soldiers with an advanced education to escape the genocide inflicted by the Khmer Rouge.

A turning point in his life came in December 1978, when Heng Cheng fully committed himself to Christ with the intention of being active in church ministries.[36] Due to the prohibition of Christianity and the intense persecution carried out by the Vietnamese, his ministry commenced in an underground setting. Frequent trips between Cambodia and Vietnam followed, as the

---

[35]International Christian Assembly Cambodia, www.ica-cambodia.org (accessed on August 21, 2016).

[36]Heng Cheng, interview by author, August 15, 2016.

remaining Khmer Christians who survived the genocide tried to secretly launch Christian networks.

Persecution by the Vietnamese intensified in the 1980s, with many Khmer Christians being imprisoned. The majority of pastors having been killed by the Khmer Rouge and most Bibles destroyed, the very thought of planting churches seemed impossible. Nevertheless, the believers continued to search for other believers so they could unite together. One strategy was to walk the streets on Sunday looking for houses and businesses with locked doors, which probably meant there were Christians inside observing the Sabbath.[37] This clever tactic demonstrated that, although the doors were locked on the outside, there was hope on the inside for Christians to join together for fellowship, prayer, and reading from likely tattered, torn pages of a Bible.

The year 1985 saw many changes as World Vision and the Overseas Missions Fellowship took the initiative to secretly distribute the New Testament among the Khmer. During that same year, Jerusalem Church was founded, with both Khmer and Vietnamese Christians meeting to have worship services together.[38] Each Sunday, the messages were preached in both languages as the believers joyfully met near the Central Market (*Psar Tmey*), yet they always maintained a watchful eye for spies and government officials.

Shortly before Jerusalem Church was associated with the AG in 1990, the newly established State of Cambodia prohibited the Khmer Christians from evangelizing but did formally recognize the Christian Church and allowed Christian gatherings.[39] Fittingly, this open door came as AG missionaries were entering the country to initiate compassion ministries. Heng Cheng and Andrew Kuong, both of whom continued to

---

[37]Ibid.

[38]Brian Maher with Uon Seila, "*Cry of the Gecko*" (Centralia, WA: Gorham Printing, 2012), 29.

[39]Heng, interview by author.

serve at Jerusalem Church throughout the 1990s, were the first pastors in Cambodia to be officially credentialed as AG ministers.

Ministry in the Provinces

The early 1990s saw additional AG missionaries come to Cambodia from the United States, France, Australia, Malaysia, and the Philippines.[40] Prior to the government elections in 1993, which was overseen by the United Nations, many limitations had been placed on Christian groups and organizations; however, provisions were granted for them to operate medical clinics and orphanages. Thus, the AG's opportunities outside Phnom Penh grew, with ministries established to the north in Kampong Cham Province, to the west in Kampong Speu Province, and to the south in Takeo Province and Kampong Som Province.

Ministry in Kampong Cham Province started to move forward in 1991 through the leadership of missionaries Steve and Jacque Sullivan. They connected with scattered believers who had come to Christ under the ministry of Christian and Missionary Alliance (CMA) leaders prior to the Khmer Rouge takeover in 1975. Just as in Phnom Penh, although meetings at that time were held in secret due to the Communist presence, special provisions had been made for the creation of compassion ministries. Because of the immense number of orphans in the country, the government made property available in Kampong Cham for the AG to build an orphanage. Widespread flooding in 1992 allowed the Sullivans to give funds to the government in order to provide for the basic needs of the people. The government showed its appreciation for the flood assistance by

---

[40]Darin Clements and Ken Huff, "The Pentecostal Movement in Cambodia," (Paper presented for the Assemblies of God Missionary Fellowship, July, 2015).

allowing a former CMA church, which was being used as military barracks, to be returned and used as a place of worship. In addition, public religious meetings, which were uncommon in Cambodia prior to the 1993 elections, were sanctioned, with the CMA conducting a Sunday service at 8:00 a.m. and the AG conducting one at 10:00 a.m.[41]

New ministries and opportunities continued in Kampong Cham Province throughout 1992. By the time missionaries Kelly and Cyndi Robinette arrived in August of that year, a nine-bed hospital with a surgery room had been constructed in Kraek and a multi-room clinic broke ground in Paouv.[42] The result in those locations eventually included the orphanage, five church plants, and opportunities for medical outreaches. Not only was God opening doors for the AG to expand in ministry, but also future Assemblies of God Cambodia (AGC) leaders would connect with those early ministries in Kampong Cham. At the orphanage, a dorm worker named Oum Rotha and an orphan named Eng Sam Ath both later became general superintendants with the AGC.[43] Also, a teenager and his family, who had come to the Kraek clinic in 1992 to receive treatment for their health needs heard the gospel. That teenager, Ath The, would later become an AGC general council committee member and dean of students at Cambodia Bible Institute in Phnom Penh.[44]

Further ministry opportunities in 1992-1993 led to establishment of an orphanage in Kampong Som Province, a clinic in Kampong Speu Province, and schools in Takeo Province. These were integral in providing a foundation for the Assemblies of God to effectively minister to immediate needs, to strategize for future possibilities, and to build key relationships with Khmer nationals. It was during this time that AG

---

[41]Kelly Robinette, interview by author, August 1, 2016.
[42]Ibid.
[43]Ibid.
[44]Ath The, interview by author, August 4, 2016.

missionaries from the Philippines and the United States invested in the lives of capable believers through discipleship and mentoring. Some of the nationals, working as staff or connected with the compassion ministries, would eventually become pastors and leaders, among them: Khek Srin, Som Pha, Khin Khon, Tun Chhay, Seing San, and Phaeng Sovan—all of whom are still active in ministry.[45]

Cambodia Bible Institute

Following Cambodia's 1993 general election, greater freedoms and liberties in regard to religion were granted, providing even more opportunities for the Assemblies of God to minister among the Khmer. Later that year, the AG pursued the establishment of an institute in Phnom Penh to train and equip church leaders and future pastors. Area Director Ron Maddux, who had made numerous trips to Cambodia after his initial visit in March 1990, was asked to teach the first course. A group of 20 Khmer and Vietnamese students gathered in a small hotel near Norodom Boulevard to participate in a course on the doctrine of the Holy Spirit.[46] This class was the beginning of the Cambodia Bible Institute (CBI).

CBI was officially founded in 1994, with a one-year training program under the leadership of Steve Sullivan (director), Fred Capapas (dean of students), and Nora Catipon (business administrator and registrar).[47] In addition to these leaders, the first teachers included Rick Shell, Jean Johnson, and Andrew Kuong. Following changes and adaptations to the curriculum, CBI developed a church-planting program in 2002. Since the Assemblies of God Cambodia (AGC) did not have an initiative

---

[45]Ken Huff, interview by author, August 8, 2016.
[46]Robinette, interview by author.
[47]Darin Clements and Ken Huff, "The Pentecostal Movement in Cambodia."

specifically focused on church planting, this program was significant in three ways: partnership with the national church, fulfillment of program requirements for graduation, and (most importantly) new churches being planted in Cambodia.[48]

Additional changes made in CBI's curriculum led to implementation of its current Associate of Arts and Bachelor of Arts programs in Bible and Church Ministries. By 2011, the Christian Life Discipleship Program had been started in Siem Reap Province and then expanded to the provinces of Kampong Thom, Battambang, and Takeo. That same year saw creation of the Christian Service Program in the Vietnamese language offered at study sites in both the capital city and surrounding areas. Overall, since the first graduating class in 1996, CBI has awarded, as of 2015, diplomas and certificates to 300 students, with many of those continuing in full-time vocational ministry among the Khmer and Vietnamese in Cambodia.

Cambodia School of Missions

Through the leadership of Filipino missionary Nora Catipon, a second AG Bible school—Cambodia School of Missions (CSM)—was founded in 2009, its main focus being the planting of new churches and cell groups. The program curriculum was designed for students to study practical ministry and Bible courses, with oversight provided for them to apply their studies throuh actual church planting endeavors.

Since its inception, 43 students have graduated from either the certificate program in ministry/missions or the diploma program in pastoral ministry. So far, those graduates have started a total of 27 churches and 25 cell groups, with the majority located in the rural, provincial areas of Cambodia. The modular approach of block courses and extended time to serve

---

[48]Darin and Dianna Clements, interview by author, August 23, 2016.

in ministry has enabled CSM to be effective both in the classroom through practical teaching and in the application of ministry connected to church planting. Flexibility within these programs allows students to study on campus in Phnom Penh for two weeks and then return to the provinces for applied ministry, which lasts some six to eight weeks.

General Council of the Assemblies of God Cambodia

Formation of the Assemblies of God Cambodia (AGC) did not occur until 1997, even though AG missionaries and ministries had been in the nation since 1990. Nevertheless, over that seven-year span, missionaries continually trained and mentored the future leaders who were integral from the beginning of the earliest ministries. It must be noted again that it was Cambodia's general elections in 1993 that opened doors for more freedom among Christians and made possible the opportunity for the government's official recognition. The year 1994 was extremely significant, as this included the first organized meetings of AG pastors and leaders, in addition to its first two ministers to be credentialed—Heng Cheng and Andrew Kuong.[49]

---

[49]Robinette, interview by author.

Chapter 2

An Analysis of the History of the Assemblies of God and Cultural Dynamics in Cambodia

The Khmer People

Khmer Culture and Worldview

A proper way to understand culture is by taking into account the values, ideas, and feelings that are associated with patterns of behavior.[1] This enables a perception about life in general, in addition to the ways that people live individually and collectively. Identifying the relevance within this fundamental area will provide insight in regard to how individuals and groups maintain their way of life, and the various means they use to cope with corresponding environments.[2]

The Khmer is the primary people group in Cambodia, comprising nearly 90% of the country's population. As previously noted regarding history, this people group can be historically traced back 2,000 years, but it was not until the early 9th century that they emerged as a dominant power. The Khmer Empire was the largest in Southeast Asia for 600 years and gradually made a shift from Hinduism as its main religion to

---

[1]Paul G. Hiebert, *Anthropological Insights for Missionaries* (Grand Rapids, MI: Baker Books, 1985), 30.

[2]Charles H. Kraft, "Culture, Worldview, and Contextualization" in *Perspectives on the World Christian Movement 4th Edition*, ed. Ralph D. Winter and Steven Hawthorne (Pasadena, CA: William Carey Library, 2009), 401.

become a Buddhist kingdom. Eventually, the Khmer and their region of Cambodia were claimed as part of French Indochina and later given their independence by France in 1953.

The decades that followed were defined by civil war, political upheaval, displacement, and ultimately genocide. The culture in Cambodia was changed as people shifted from a collective mindset to a more individualistic one. Each person fought for his own survival instead of relying on group association. In spite of various coping methods, this tragic chapter of Cambodian history still lives on for the Khmer as well as their culture. In more modern times, there appears to be a pervasive sense of advancement for those born after the civil war and genocide. However, these sentiments are commonly obscured among those who endured the tragedies of the 1970s. Identity issues, depression, and post-traumatic stress disorder continue to plague many of these individuals as they attempt to handle past events.[3]

In the midst of continually rebuilding the country, coupled with the pains of the past decades, the Khmer stand as a unique people group. The major aspect in understanding them is to recognize the significance of their previous empire, catastrophes of war and genocide, optimism among the young generation, and enduring traditions. A key characteristic of their culture that stands out today is the importance they place on togetherness. Their expressions and orientations show how they find satisfaction by simply sharing life with others and maintaining meaningful relationships.[4]

When observing worldview from an anthropological perspective, it is important to comprehend the assumptions,

---

[3]Seanglim Bit, *The Warrior Heritage: A Psychological Perspective of Cambodian Trauma* (El Cerrito, CA: Seanglim Bit, 1991), 118.

[4]Sherwood G. Lingenfelter and Marvin K. Mayers, *Ministering Cross-Culturally: An Incarnational Model for Personal Relationships*,(Grand Rapids, MI: Baker Books, 1986), 83.

allegiances, and values that comprise a people group's perception of reality and how that group responds accordingly.[5] The incorporation of how a people group views reality, in addition to the associated assumptions, plays a significant role within its thought processes, which are related to natural life and the supernatural. Moreover, the way people view themselves and their perceptions of environment are essential to ideas being either embraced or rejected.[6] As for Southeast Asia, and specifically in Cambodia, worldview is acknowledged to be deeply integrated into the cultural composition.

It is necessary to understand worldview and its overall significance among the Khmer, as it is likened to a type of guide related to how people live and the ways it brings culture together into a single design.[7] The predominant Buddhist worldview in Southeast Asia is clearly exemplified by the Khmer, because it is deeply integrated in their culture. The assumptions and perceptions that encompass worldview show that the Khmer see their lives in a cyclical manner. Reality to them is something that can be deemed as beyond their own control, and they recognize that environment involves the supernatural rather than the natural.[8] General qualities associated with life in Cambodia are seen as being intertwined with suffering and with the uncertainty of having a clear comprehension of reality.

---

[5]Charles H. Kraft, *Anthropology for Christian Witness* (Maryknoll, NY: Orbis Books, 1996), 52.

[6]David J. Hesselgrave and Edward Rommen, *Contextualization* (Pasadena, CA: William Carey Library, 1989), 212.

[7]Paul G. Hiebert, *Anthropological Insights for Missionaries*, 48.

[8]Charles H. Kraft, *Christianity with Power* (Grand Rapids, MI: Servant Books, 1989), 88.

Leadership Patterns from Angkor

The era of Angkor signified a mighty empire that dominated much of Southeast Asia for six centuries. Its former power is reflected in the stone buildings that remain, and its legacy continually declares itself to all passing visitors who make their way to Siem Reap to behold the temples firsthand. While these looming ruins also speak of the empire's defeat, decline, and decay, they continue to tell the story of the renowned kings who exercised their authority over peoples and regions. Leadership was demonstrated through the absolute authority of a single, ruling individual.

The kings of the Khmer Empire were revered and hailed to the highest level due to their regality. They were also noted to have supernatural power, which enabled the continuance of the empire.[9] Furthermore, life was lived by positioning oneself in the most advantageous way in order to preserve and maintain existence. Those who lived during that particular epoch in history were subjects with a dispositional alignment to their authoritative ruler.[10] These axioms were acknowledged as a common part of life during the Khmer Empire, due to the regal greatness exhibited and paraded before the masses, plus the reverent submission on behalf of the subjects.

The kings who established, and expanded, the empire were viewed as ultimate, powerful beings responsible for mediating in both earthly and spiritual matters.[11] Although their position could be challenged by opposing kings from other regions, their overall standing included a view which proceeded downward to the dependent beings below them. On the other hand, the people lived at the benevolence of their ruler yet understood this

---

[9]David P. Chandler, *The Land and People of Cambodia*, 59.
[10]David P. Chandler, *A History of Cambodia*, 2nd Ed., 47.
[11]Seanglim Bit, *The Warrior Heritage*, 18.

standing to be advantageous, with the prospect of being perpetual beneficiaries. Their view was upward, as it demonstrated willful capitulation in addition to solidifying their position of service.

Aspects of supreme leadership, and conformity to that leadership, laid a foundation among the Khmer that has demonstrated repetition throughout each generation. Even though varied kings and leaders have used authority via the means of suppression, the people instinctively gravitate toward rule of this nature. The stance is one not of adulation but comprehended from the standpoint of "feasible continuance." Moreover, governance by the absolute leader in Cambodia has been commonly seen to preserve stability and maintain control in the most effective way.

There is a distinct dichotomy in Cambodia among those who are designated as leaders and those who are situated below the leaders. Whether from the stately government offices in Phnom Penh or a rural church in the provincial countryside, authority is vested in the manner of control due to allegiances and patron-client relationships. Cambodian society falls in line with this rationale, as control is predominately demonstrated by maintaining order, which enables the leaders to rule according to their personal prerogative and the populace being merely sustained. This creates a hierarchy among the Khmer that encapsulates the very nature of society and reveals the overall framework related to the important areas of status and role.

Societal Implications

Within cultural areas connected to societal implications in Cambodia, status and role are among the most significant. Recognition of one's position in society, as well as the various behavior patterns associated with that particular position, will create the framework of how culture operates both individually and collectively.[12] The necessity of observing status and role and the way in which they are portrayed among the Khmer, show how they are intrinsically linked with relationships. From the Angkor era until the present time, the Khmer have continually identified themselves in regard to their own position of status and how it relates to others within their own people group.[13]

Whereas status relates to the overall structure of society and entails one's identity, position, and assigned duties, a person's role is the behavior of status and is recognized as the foremost component.[14] Status for individuals can be noted as the way they are identified within society and how others view them. This demonstrates a structure within which each person lives and operates among others, in addition to the general arrangement of the expectations that are set before people. On the other hand, role is the function of individuals within their status and can be seen as the dynamic feature of societal behavior.[15] Since status and role have direct integrations within a particular society, this brings an interconnection in relationships, which can focus on how each person is identified and performs.

There is a definite hierarchy as it correlates to status among the Khmer. One prime example is the terminology in the Khmer language that relates to how people address one another. Communication within relationships has separate forms to designate people by their social ranking, age, and occupation that provides structure and clarity as it pertains to status.[16] In regard to roles in Cambodia, each person is expected to be responsible to maintain the status quo within his status as it relates to how he is viewed in society, family, and work. A

---

[12]Paul G. Hiebert, *Anthropological Insights for Missionaries,* 256.
[13]Seanglim Bit, *The Warrior Heritage,* 22.
[14]Charles H. Kraft, *Anthropology for Christian Witness,* 314-315.
[15]Ibid., 315.
[16]Seanglim Bit, *The Warrior Heritage,* 22.

significant societal feature among the Khmer has to do with the authority ascribed within status and how that authority is exhibited through various roles. Even though the societal composition of the Khmer strives to maintain balance and harmony, authority is commonly used through various roles to control and coerce others.[17]

One final aspect of statuses and roles in Khmer society to be noted is the overall association with Buddhism in Cambodia. Due to its overarching presence, everyone accepts who they are in their status, and what is expected of them through their role, since all levels of existence are related within *samsara* (i.e., the wheel/cycle of life). Existence is not seen as a matter of moving up or down, because life has already been predetermined through the nature of karma and how a person has responded in their previous lives. The Khmer recognize where they are and maintain their position through merit, which is recognized as life here and now. That proceeds to drive karma, which ultimately drives *samsara*.

Patron-Client Analysis

The relationship between patrons and clients brings cohesion because it provides stability and security for individuals, the group, and society at large.[18] It is seen as a basic necessity in many countries where those with means and authority are able to make provision, which brings support from others while maintaining valuable relationships. Societies with patronage systems abound throughout the world, and the networks within various cultures intrinsically link individuals. Not only is patronage present within general work, but it can be noted in various facets in which relationships demonstrate a

---

[17]Ibid., 61.
[18]Paul G. Hiebert, *Anthropological Insights for Missionaries*, 124.

hierarchy of authority and people who entrust themselves to those who maintain power. One specific aspect is the area of politics, where authority is present in a visible way and can develop into a long-term relationship with all parties finding benefits.[19]

Although the specific details of patron-client relationships cannot be fully proven throughout Khmer history, various evidences demonstrate similarities that established, and continues, this type of relationship. Once again, authority was the deciding factor, because it was enacted through the behavior of leaders and rulers. This is aligned with status and role in societies where visible power is displayed not only through authority, but also through the power of influence.[20] A hierarchy of this particular nature progressed through the various eras of Cambodia and continues within the modern relationships of the Khmer.

The instability that has plagued Cambodia for centuries is a major contributing factor in causing the people to be in constant search of those who can ensure provision and stability at the most opportune time. The changes and tragedies this country has endured, the significance of status and role within society, and the value placed on relationships have combined to allow the patron-client model to be quite suitable in Cambodia. Overall, this system among the Khmer situates bonds similar to parent-child and older sibling-younger siblings, all the while maintaining a responsible, protective function that yields mutual benefits.[21]

---

[19]www.emqonline.com/node/2162 (accessed on August 28, 2016).
[20]Charles H. Kraft, *Anthropology for Christian Witness*, 321.
[21]Seanglim Bit, *The Warrior Heritage*, 69-70.

From Collectivism to Individualism

The decades prior to the civil war and genocide displayed the Khmer as people living in a collective sense, with individuals closely linked to one another. Cambodia was understood to exhibit trust, stability, and balance within relationships and the overall framework of society. The majority of Khmer lived and worked in the provincial countryside, with the harvest of rice acknowledged as the primary source pf personal income and the country's sustainability. Life was simple yet structured. The children were taught by monks at the Buddhist temples in order to receive education and a rich understanding of their culture.[22] Families and villages were based upon togetherness, which kept Cambodia going in the proper direction in spite of being a third-world country. By the time of independence from France in 1953, Phnom Penh was steadily growing, and the people in the capital city started to see development and progress within a growing urban class. These "new people," as the Khmer Rouge would later call them, were targeted and viewed as disposable, since educated and urban individuals failed to line up with extreme Marxism.[23]

During the reign of the Khmer Rouge, their cadres believed that elimination of the previous society could produce necessary change. So, a new form of collectivism was established by the separation of families, the removal of education, and prohibitions on religion.[24] Not only was there a removal of relationship, but the language distinctions used to acknowledge one another by status were eliminated and replaced by a word for designating a common friend—*mitt*.

---

[22]David P. Chandler, *The Tragedy of Cambodian History*, 89.
[23]David P. Chandler, *The Land and People of Cambodia*, 149.
[24]Seanglim Bit, *The Warrior Heritage*, 46.

Furthermore, the people were told that the *Angkar* (i.e., organization) was the new family that provided life within collectivism. All previous aspects of family were eradicated, as people were not only removed from their loved ones, but also encouraged to spy on one another and report even the slightest infractions.[25] This new foundation of camaraderie was based upon an increase in rice production for an agrarian society that would supply the industrialization needed for advancement.

The Khmer Rouge emphasized collectivism to the point of executing individuals who foraged food, because this was seen as opposition to the new authority.[26] This overarching structure led to strict discouragement of individualism; however, individualism was the main method of survival for those who labored in the fields since society had been torn asunder. Countless hours of working in the fields while being surrounded by death taught people that to place hope in *Angka* led to destruction, but letting go of everything and striving forward as an individual brought survival.[27]

Disfigured Collectivism

The principle of individualism to merely survive was still being lived out after the Vietnamese invasion in 1979. When the country was reformed in 1989, people tried to find ways of reintegrating their lives into collective living. The country as a whole struggled to return to collectivism because most features of society still functioned under the premise of individualism. Various shifts from having togetherness to being broken apart through genocide with collectivism based upon extreme

---

[25]Evan Gottesman, *Cambodia After the Khmer Rouge* (New Haven, CT: Yale University Press, 2003), 87.
[26]Randle C. DeFalco, "Justice and Starvation in Cambodia: The Khmer Rouge Famine" in *The Cambodia Law and Policy Journal* 2 (2014): 53.
[27]Don Cormack, *Killing Fields, Living Fields*, 188.

Communism ultimately led people living in a to survival mode. As the Khmer slowly rebuilt their lives and the country as a whole, collectivism returned but with numerous flaws. These changes left Cambodia in a status that can be best describes as "disfigured collectivism."

Prior elements of trust, balance, and stability were inevitably replaced by suspicion, fear, and dependency in the 1980s and 1990s. Those who studied the crisis in Cambodia quickly saw the fragility among the people, as widespread poverty, lack of infrastructure, and rampant corruption filled the country.[28] The people could simply not trust each other or work together, as the country was rebuilt by a society still living to survive day by day and looking out only for themselves. Furthermore, the next generation of children and youth saw their upbringings radically altered due to the fallout effects of the Khmer Rouge. Countless children were orphaned due to the genocide, and former teenage soldiers who had been taught to change the "old ways" of the country would forever live with guilt for killing countless countrymen.[29]

Religion in Cambodia

Buddhist Patterns and Practices

The Khmer identify themselves through association with Theravada Buddhism as demonstrated in a common statement: "To be Cambodian is to be Buddhist." However, the beliefs and practices that are applied could be best described as "folk Buddhism," containing various elements of Buddhism, Hinduism, and animism. This conglomeration that is

---

[28]David P. Chandler, *The Land and People of Cambodia,* 187.
[29]David P. Chandler, *The Tragedy of Cambodian History,* 243.

acknowledged as religion is accepted by the people, but the meanings are generally unknown.

For missionaries serving in Cambodia, Khmer perceptions and patterns are commonly seen firsthand. These convey the overall Khmer worldview and how it makes a unique impression on customs, structures, and life in general. The practices of Theravada Buddhism in Cambodia place an enormous emphasis upon each individual, his personal quest to identify suffering, and ways to break free from that suffering. All facets within this particular framework keep this worldview at the innermost part of each person while avoiding acknowledgement of any specific deity. Furthermore, innate attitudes and human-based suppositions are ultimately dictated by a worldview that traps people in a cycle that only remains inward.[30]

Analyzing the intricate details of Khmer culture and worldview in association with Buddhism demonstrates how religious patterns are connected with both individuals and groups through beliefs and practices. Although the norm in Cambodia is association with Theravada Buddhism, the primary religious patterns take on the animistic characteristics of folk Buddhism. Basic inclinations among the Khmer are seen to be practical for their day-to-day life rather than trying to provide answers to questions deemed as unnecessary.

A challenge to understanding the religious patterns of the Khmer involves a comprehension of the various folk beliefs and practices that have roots in either Hinduism or animism and were gradually transferred into Buddhism.[31] Whether it is the reverence of a supernatural being near a home (neak ta), the celebration of the Pchum Ben festival as a way to assist deceased

---

[30]Larry L. Niemeyer, *Cultural Anthropology: Cultural Studies for Ministry Practitioners: Readings and Resource Materials* (Springfield, MO: Global University, 2006), 103.

[31]Saw Allen, Russell H. Bowers, Jr., and Dilani Senapatiratne, *Folk Buddhism in Southeast Asia* (Phnom Penh, Cambodia: Training of Timothys, 2003), 49.

ancestors, or visiting a shaman *(kru Khmer)* to obtain guidance, there is one pervasive element that seems to drive people and their patterns—fear! Many people groups in Southeast Asia function this way, which seems to be dominated by continual focus on the activity of spirits (both good and bad), in addition to the ways and means to give appeasement that enables security.[32] The Khmer are no exception as they follow in the same manner.

Religious patterns involving Buddhism in Cambodia are strongly connected to the Khmer worldview and remain deeply integrated in the culture of who they are as a people group. Comprehending the particular contexts of their beliefs as well as fear-driven impulses can enable outsiders to perceive where the Khmer place themselves in the journey of life.[33] Although Theravada Buddhism will always have its place within the big picture of existence, life issues will consistently be maintained through animistic means. Taking into account these beliefs and practices, whether Buddhist or animistic, coupled with their worldview enables a better perception of religion in Cambodia.

The Assemblies of God and its Significance in Cambodia

1990-1993—The Birth Years

The years following the genocide left millions displaced, and there were still thousands in refugee camps along the Thai border when the first AG resident missionaries arrived in June 1990. With desperate needs filling Cambodia, the possibility of ministering to those needs gave the AG an open door to serve among the Khmer. The most important basis of ministry was

---

[32]Marguerite G. Kraft, *Understanding Spiritual Power: A Forgotten Dimension of Cross-Cultural Mission and Ministry* (Maryknoll, NY: Orbis Books, 1995), 76.

[33]Saw Allen, Russell H. Bowers, Jr., and Dilani Senapatiratne, 65.

due to the Cambodian government asking for assistance from Christian groups and other non-government organizations (NGOs).

Because there were few buildings that could be used to provide relief, medical care, and education, the AG was able, by partnering with the government, to establish a base of ministry through compassion efforts. Although the needs at that time were so widespread and the long-term results difficult to ascertain, nevertheless many lives were touched, and dependency issues did not cause long-term complications.[34] Not only was the AG's compassion ministries platform welcomed by the Khmer, but it was able to impact key regions in Cambodia as well as shape the next several years of ministry.

As the orphanages, English-language training centers, and medical clinics were started, the missionaries envisioned eventually filling the pulpits of the new church plants with former orphans, English Second Language (ESL)-trained students, and medical patients from these various compassion ministries.[35] That visionary strategy proved significant, as many Khmer were reached in various parts of the country. Also, many were returned to their home provinces and villages bringing with them the gospel message. Equally important, many of the staff members and workers within these compassion projects became Christians and were subsequently trained as pastors and leaders.[36]

In the years prior to the nation's general election in 1993, there were many restrictions on what the missionaries could do through the means of traditional church ministries. Despite the limitations, they made the most of each situation, launching substantial compassion ministries to meet the needs of the

---

[34]Huff, interview by author, August 8, 2016.
[35]Robinette, interview by author.
[36]Huff, interview by author.

people.[37] Also, these early developmental years fostered better relations with government officials due to the fact that the AG partnered directly with them. Lastly, as individuals came to Christ, they were mentored by the missionaries and became an integral part of the overall ministry within the AG. Paradigms of this nature proved to be effective with long-term ramifications.

There were some situations during those early years, however, in which structure had not been methodically planned and thus posed possible dilemmas. For instance, there were isolated incidents of AG compassion ministries' workers trying too quickly to plant new churches without proper missiology.[38] One example involved some cross-cultural workers who came to Cambodia to serve in a medical capacity but assisted church plants; their non-contextualized approach aimed to make churches more Western rather than having a Khmer identity. But in the main, the churches planted during those initial years did move forward with the assistance of missionaries and national leaders. This was crucial as the 1993 general elections gave more freedom to Christians and allowed the AG to solidify its place and plan for future ministries.

Overall, the early years of the AG in Cambodia demonstrated the tenacity of missionaries who were willing to make the most of a challenging time. Ministry was truly limited due to the political climate and the government-decreed restrictions. Nevertheless, it is evident that God was working through those first missionaries, as well as those national leaders whom the missionaries trained and mentored. The foundation through compassion ministries was essential, as it allowed initial strategies within that realm to develop into starting a national church.

---

[37]Ath The, interview by author.
[38]Robinette, interview by author.

1994-1998—Some Firsts Within the Fellowship

The year 1994 was one of the most significant in the history of the AG in Cambodia, with various precedents established that allowed the Fellowship to move forward in both ministry and purpose. Missionaries and national pastors started to have a more outward focus, in part as a result of expanded freedoms being granted by the Cambodian government. In addition, compassion ministries continued, along with a driving initiative on church planting, expanding evangelism, and training leaders.[39]

Launching of the Cambodia Bible Institute (CBI) in 1994 brought many new possibilities for future ministry growth. For example, its first few years saw numerous students from Takeo Province, which is located to the south of Phnom Penh. Many of those CBI-trained students returned to their villages to assist in the various already-existing ministries and to plant churches. This resulted in many others from Takeo Province attending CBI and following in their predecessors' footsteps.

Within the Assemblies of God Missionary Fellowship (AGMF), the missionaries saw CBI as a major focus for ministry, as perhaps the best way to maintain relationships with national pastors, and as a primary opportunity to expand in ministry, especially church planting. This trend continued as missionaries from other countries came to Cambodia to be involved in training leaders via teaching Bible, theology, and ministry courses at CBI. Furthermore, a special partnership between the school's missionary leadership and the Khmer leaders enabled further expansion of ministry, as the missionaries trained pastors who would serve the national church in the ensuing years.

---

[39]Robinette, interview by author.

Another major event in 1994 involved the organization and structure of pastors that established a process by which missionaries and national leaders would walk alongside one another.[40] These organizational meetings were seen as significant times for the Fellowship as the Assemblies of God Cambodia (AGC) started to take shape. Not only were the first AG pastors in Cambodia credentialed, but also other leaders who had been working with missionaries assumed even more responsibilities as future ministries were planned. It was truly a process of learning and moving forward as a Fellowship, with mutual encouragement from missionaries and pastors.[41]

During this 1994-1998 period, Christianity was finally rebounding after the devastation of war and genocide. It was a time for unification, as various denominations received official recognition from the government, the Evangelical Fellowship of Cambodia (EFC) was created, and advancements were made in Bible translation. Most importantly, the number of churches grew to over 500 and the number of Christians to approximately 20,000.[42] Up until 1997, there were more Khmer churches outside Cambodia than inside the country. Thousands of Christians had left during the 1980s and planted Khmer congregations elsewhere, including the United States, Canada, France, and Australia.[43] This changed as phenomenal growth spread throughout Cambodia in cities and villages alike.

Also, this four-year period among the AG missionaries and the AGC was seen as a relationship similar to that between

---

[40]Eng Sam Ath, interviewed by author, August 10, 2016.

[41]Eng, interview by author.

[42]Cambodian Christian.com. Church History – Chronology of the Cambodian Christian Church,www.cambodianchristian.com/church_history_p5.htm (accessed September 12, 2016).

[43]Steven John Hyde, "A Missiological and Critical Study of Cambodia's Historical, Cultural, and Sociopolitical Characteristics to Identify the Factors of Rapid Church Growth and Propose its Future Prognosis" (PhD diss, Bethany International University, 2015), 66.

parents and their children.[44] It was a time of nurturing and encouragement, as the missionaries provided the necessary structure to formally create the AGC in 1997. However, in the midst of this advancement, some political challenges arose that impacted the internal composition of the Fellowship. On the negative side, no new pastors were being ordained or receiving full recognition by the AGC, even though the first ordination had occurred in 1994. The lapse from 1995-1999 demonstrated political misunderstandings and a slight stagnation in regard to the episcopacy of the AGC. This pattern was repeated later as ministers had to wait several years before they could be credentialed. A primary reason was related to changes in leadership within AGC's executive committee, which resulted in variations on those who could be officially recognized as AG ministers. Also, weaknesses regarding the administrative structure led to ambiguity in the necessary qualifications for credentialing.

1999-2008—Challenges Amidst Growth

The first eight years of the AG in Cambodia was marked by significant growth. as missionaries served with pastors in compassion ministries, founded a Bible school, formalized the general council, and planted churches. In spite of government-imposed limitations of religious freedom, the AG nevertheless built relationships with the government in order to start vital compassion ministries in the country. The strategies formed within those ministries led to new churches and capable national leaders. However, the following eight years witnessed various challenges. Since the first eight years were formative and

---

[44]Clements, interview by author.

foundational, the next eight years proved to be a period of growing pains within the Fellowship.[45]

There were genuine ministry intentions when the Community Health Evangelism (CHE) projects started in 1999. The AGC leadership recognized the potential of serving through rural development initiatives to meet the day-to-day needs of the people. It was generally agreed that providing resources through social programs would allow the Fellowship to have a proper framework, rather than approaching a village chief with empty hands.[46] So as the AGC moved forward, AG missionaries from the United States and France assisted in the rural development strategies and operations.

Within any type of ministry or mission's effort, money can be seen as a great multiplier but also can be seen as a great divider. Such was the case with the CHE programs that were launched in the provinces. While the funds within those programs enabled the general framework to expand as people were impacted through social ministries, division arose in 2004 when CHE turned into an NGO known as Cambodia Global Action (CGA). Although part of the AG, the national church ministries in the AGC, and the rural development programs in CGA, rather than being joined together, ran parallel, with the only intersection being reoccurring disagreements related to authority and finances. While the CGA had abundant funds and resources at its disposal, it was the AGC that played a more significant role despite minimal funds for its daily operation.[47]

Another predicament, in addition to those related to authority and finances, was the overall ministry approaches of the two entities. The AGC's role, as the national church, was to minister to the spiritual needs in Cambodia, whereas the CGA

---

[45]Ibid.
[46]Eng, interview by author.
[47]Ath The, interview by author.

focused on programs. The community assessments and village projects that dealt with health and agriculture administered by the CGA were enterprises that involved power and influence. So, in essence, the dividing issue came down to one of people versus programs. Thus, the challenge to be addressed was this— the AGC churches' ministry efforts would serve people's spiritual needs, whereas CGA's programs by themselves would serve only the people's physical needs.[48]

While the village programs were intended to assist people in ways such as gardening, raising livestock, and digging wells, the long-term impacts of these efforts (either socially or spiritually) were minimal. Due to the Khmer's understanding of exhibiting strong leadership (an authoritative trait seen for centuries in Cambodia), both sides of leadership in the AGC and CGA felt their decisions were the most advantageous. This conflict continued for several years because these arenas involved authority, finances, and approaches in ministry.

Another challenge during this timeframe concerned ideological differences that existed among missionaries. The Assemblies of God Missionary Fellowship (AGMF) always strived for a balanced, working relationship among missionaries, in addition to serving with the national church. However, there were many difficulties within the AGMF in the late 1990s and early 2000s due to conflicts of interest regarding how the missionaries should serve, especially in relationship with the AGC. Disagreements in missiology and strategy for the future led to a problematic cycle for several years, which ultimately caused instability. Some of the leaders abused their power and overstepped boundaries by trying to supervise the ministries of the AGC. Power struggles were not uncommon, even leading to a situation in which one missionary decided to

---

[48]Eng, interview by author.

personally confer ministerial credentials to 12 national pastors without involvement of the AGC or the AGMF.

Missionary leadership went through several changes during this period. A board of missionary representatives from France, the United States, Australia, and the Philippines was formed to provide stability on the field and approval for ministry projects. However, the hoped-for camaraderie and cooperation remained quite distant and ultimately resulted in the departure of several missionaries from the field. One major issue involved the decision for the International Christian Assembly (ICA) to partner with Cambodia Bible Institute (CBI) to construct a new facility. The plan was to build it on the CBI campus with adequate space for CBI, ICA, and AGMF offices and classrooms. Although the plan was ultimately successful, again, the conflicts of interest led to internal problems among missionary leaders, which caused additional strife and division.

Of course, there were some positives realized during this otherwise difficult period, one of which involved a church planting program at CBI in the early 2000s. The program curriculum required the students to plant a church, or start a cell group, as a condition for graduation. Although not all of the churches were considered sovereign, it is estimated that 20 new churches were planted between 2002 and 2005.[49] This was quite significant in light of the fact that the AGC did not have a church-planting program during that time.

In summary, the years 1999-2008 should serve as a reminder of the importance of relationships, since such can greatly advance or greatly weaken any fellowship. Philosophical differences, power struggles, and the manipulation of fellow workers—all can limit growth in the midst of great potential. One particularly unfortunate result for the AG in Cambodia was the attrition rate among appointed AG missionaries, as both

---

[49]Clements, interview by author.

veterans and first-termers left Cambodia due to differences in ideologies and conflicts with one another. Scars still remain because of those conflicts, and some of the issues have still to be resolved. Furthermore, the various situations that led to attrition not only resulted in some missionaries leaving the field, but also caused some ministries to cease, with no personnel to maintain the roles that had been established.[50]

2009-2015—Resourcing the Fellowship

The years following those internal challenges saw positive changes in the relationship between the AG missionaries and the AGC pastors. Whereas in the early 1990s (when the missionaries had assumed leadership roles to guide the fellowship), as the national leaders were being trained, in the era from 2009-2015, the missionaries became partners with the national leaders and served as needed within the various ministries and programs. In other words, prior roles that were once parent-child had now become older sibling-younger sibling, the result being that relationships turned more positive as resourcing the Fellowship was mutually understood as a major component.[51]

Regarding relationships among AG missionaries, harmony was evident as those on the field put the challenging years behind them to focus on ways to serve the AGC. Solid leadership at all levels (e.g., country moderators, leadership teams, country representatives) set a tone that promoted greater cooperation and cohesion in the Fellowship. This demonstration of unity eventually led to a joint AG Missionary Fellowship Conference in 2014, which was held in Kampong Som Province. It was the first gathering of this kind in over 15 years, with eight countries being represented. Although there were still differences with

---

[50]Ann Greve, interview by author, August 31, 2016.
[51]Clements, interview by author.

regard to missiology and philosophical tenets, the main focus among AG missionaries was to move in the right direction together, with the goal of open, continual partnership with the AGC.

A primary challenge the AGC faced was related to mother churches maintaining daughter churches and cell groups. This led to some relationship problems within the development of sovereign congregations and internal growth that could result in an overall weak structure. Thus, although growth did occur between the years 2009 and 2015, it tended to be wider and more shallow than deep and substantive.[52] The solution could have been provided through a greater focus on discipleship. Those congregations, house churches, and small groups in the AGC that had demonstrated significant potential viewed discipleship as a way to enrich the lives of their members. It must be noted that CBI started the Christian Life Program during this time, in order to provide assistance in the area of church discipleship. The implication of recognizing the "depth issues" within local churches allowed missionaries and pastors alike to address weaknesses in an advantageous way.

Finances and money were still ongoing concerns for both the AGC and the CGA from 2009 to 2015. Christian seminars and conferences became extremely popular both inside and outside Cambodia. The CGA, with its larger budget, was able to provide for its staff to attend these meetings, while AGC pastors and leadership were struggling to maintain the well-being of their churches. The pattern of programs in the CGA versus the spiritual concerns in the AGC tended to keep both sides distant and moving in parallel due to their differing visions and strategies. It can be surmised from the activities and attitudes that, although there were sincere intentions to focus outward, the general results were lacking in regard to the potential.

---

[52]Huff, interview by author.

One of the more positive aspects of the AGC was addressed in 2010, its structure being of concern. The organization of districts in the national church allowed for associations and partnerships among the pastors and leaders to be taken to a higher level. This was a necessary strategy for ministry, since each district was now able to focus on specific regions and still remain part of the big picture within the AGC. In addition, decisions made within these structures enabled a clearer realization of partnership within close proximities and expansion within the Fellowship. The promoting of various ministries in the districts enabled those gifted in specific areas (e.g. youth, children, adults) to have a greater impact in both small district settings and the Fellowship as a whole. Moreover, it allowed the missionaries to serve within the AGC by building relationships with pastors in different locations.

Lastly, during the 2009-2015 period, positive changes were made to the AGC's constitution that coincided with assisting pastors and those desiring to receive recognition in the fellowship. One was the change to have an annual general council, which brought many positive results, among them—strong attendance, unified committees, open discussions, and solidarity among pastors and missionaries. Another change was the expansion to multiple levels of credentials and recognition services for those receiving credentials. Both of these changes have enhanced the structure within the national church and provided a stronger standing for the AG in Cambodia.

Chapter 3

An Analysis of the
Missions Practices Used and
Projections for the Future

Insights for Missionaries in Cambodia

Initial Approaches to Understanding Worldview and Religion

Within the realm of cross-cultural ministry, there are countless paradigms that have proven to be successful or contain moderate results or fail altogether in regard to effective engagement within a particular region. Although this immense area of ministry seems to have a myriad of strategies, the overall emphasis and effectiveness can have sharpened focus by understanding the worldview and religion of those served. Such is essential for missionaries in a cross-cultural setting such as Cambodia as the missionaries utilize their areas of strength, improve their areas of weakness, and endeavor to be more effective in their calling. Recent statistics reveal that while the Khmer comprise nearly 90% of Cambodia's population, only 1.7% identify as evangelical Christians.[1] Thus, the Khmer are a people group waiting to hear an adequate presentation of the gospel and must rely (unknowingly) on those who fully comprehend these fundamental aspects.

---

[1]Joshua Project. Cambodia, www.joshuaproject.net/countries/CB (accessed on October 15, 2016).

As we recognize the implications of valuable approaches within missions, we must narrow our focus from the outset. The foundation should begin by recognizing the perceptions and practices that make up any particular people group. This will bring understanding to the surface of our approaches and enable cross-cultural workers to develop methods deemed as valuable and comprehensive. Missionaries serving in Cambodia are no exception, thus they must strive to recognize Cambodians'' worldview components in addition to the intricacies of religion among the Khmer.

It is necessary for missionaries to understand the distinctions within Cambodians' worldview and religion by looking below the surface to the primary beliefs, as well as to the related behavior that follows.[2] Although the world is rapidly changing even among Buddhists in Southeast Asia, there are key components within their lives that will never change. Missionaries must recognize those areas that have remained the same for multiple generations, and take into account the resulting structure of religion that provides comfort, purpose, and meaning in daily life.[3] For missionaries who are beginning their ministry in Cambodia, it is especially important that they strive to see how Cambodians' worldview must be continually addressed within a Buddhist context, while assessing areas that are immovable, and aspects that may change.

The basic notions of Buddhism are essentially a self-salvific philosophy with a minimal concept of an almighty, sovereign God.[4] Offerings for monks are given in order to receive merit for one's self, prayers are merely positive confessions towards

---

[2]R. Daniel Shaw and Charles E. Van Engen, *Communicating God's Word in a Complex World: God's Truth or Hocus Pocus?* (Oxford, UK: Rowman & Littlefield Publishers, Inc., 2003), 140.

[3]Gailyn Van Rheenen, "A Theology of Power," *Evangelical Missions Quarterly* 41 (2005): 32.

[4]Tissa Weerasingha, "Karma and Christ: Opening Our Eyes to the Buddhist World," *International Journal of Frontier Missions* 10 (1993), 103.

self, and honoring ancestors provides solace on behalf of self. There are definite religious issues to note in Cambodia that can be either deeply rooted within their worldview, or on the surface of an individual's beliefs. Two common areas among the Khmer are the concept of God and patterns of syncretism.

Even if individuals gradually accept the concept of God in a general sense, the aspect of God being distant causes immediate problems in their understanding. For Khmer Buddhists, their rationale could ultimately lead them to a place of recognizing God's existence, yet viewing him as limited and unable to assist with the problems of life. Concepts related to God, such as his preexistence and the story of creation have been shown to be effective among the Khmer, as those areas can be related to their worldview and religion, as well as to confronting barriers in the most appropriate way. An example of this is demonstrated in the *Book of Hope*, which is distributed among young people in Cambodia. One major part in the book focuses on the creation account and has brought many people to an understanding of God and his creative work.

As concerning syncretism, numerous people groups in Southeast Asia tend to combine various beliefs and practices in order to cope with everyday problems.[5] This commonly occurs among the Khmer, and poses a danger of mixing elements of Christianity with previously established practices. Unless recognized and handled immediately, potential believers in Christ can be susceptible to simply adding Christianity to their present system in order to enhance their own rituals.[6] Missionaries can properly address aspects connected to syncretism through clear communication with, and oversight of, believers while taking into account the characteristics of Cambodians' worldview.

---

[5]David Burnett, *The Spirit of Buddhism*, (London, UK: Monarch Books, 1996), 116.
[6]Charles H. Kraft, "Culture, Worldview, and Contextualization," 405.

Although varying changes occur within worldview and religion, the inclusion of new ideas and patterns may bring resistance, which will eventually turn into barriers within a particular people group's worldview.[7] The traditional way of perceptions and practices within a worldview gives stability and maintains familiarity, thereby providing individuals with both personal and collective assurances. When change occurs, even on a small scale, in something seen as regular and commonplace, the result can be a strain due to the fact that traditions have strong connections within a worldview.[8] Allegiances can be viewed with doubt whenever an individual demonstrates even the slightest inclination to change, since such a change is seen as abandonment of key aspects connected to that worldview.

In a sense, a Khmer individual who willfully ventures into the realm of change within an established system is making the decision to forego his identity. This particular issue is significant to distinguish in Cambodia, as it pertains to allegiances to the overall religious system, and calls into question the loyalty that one will have among his own people.[9] Rejecting identity, in addition to embracing change considered to be disruptive to worldview are perceived as the common result for those who accept Christ and leave the path of Buddhism. This should cause missionaries in Cambodia to realize how God can use people by natural means to reveal himself supernaturally in ways that are not confined to worldview or religion.[10]

In summary, one of the most vital aspects within missions is to comprehend the worldview and religion of the people groups being served. This is the foundation for all missiological areas, since it relates to unreached peoples, in addition to their perceptions and practices. From the onset of cross-cultural

---

[7]Paul G. Hiebert, *Anthropological Insights for Missionaries*, 49.
[8]Charles H. Kraft, *Anthropology for Christian Witness*, 380.
[9]Ibid., 200.
[10]Larry L. Niemeyer, *Cultural Anthropology*, 107.

ministry in Cambodia, missionaries must examine their approaches by learning and applying that knowledge in a correct context. This means taking into consideration the nuances and barriers of Buddhism and Khmer worldview.

The Khmer have suffered as a people group, especially in recent decades, in regard to war and genocide. Their perceptions and practices continue to be both practical and survival-orientated, because these align with the suffering they have endured.[11] For the missionary who learns and applies that knowledge in this manner, there will be not only greater insight and understanding, but also more effective results among the Khmer. Such appropriate learning and application can be initiated by acclimation of language and culture, continual dialogue with those who have extensive cross-cultural experience, and striving to build relationships with nationals.

Relationship with the National Church

"We still have missionaries here, and they are just like God. We know they exist, but we never see them."[12] These frightening words describe an all-too-common situation in regard to missionaries in a cross-cultural setting who fail to effectively serve with the national church. It is simply not enough for them to learn another language, comprehend people groups and their respective worldviews, adjust to cultural differences, and engage in various ministries. It is partnership with the national church that must be implemented in order to see positive results.

When AG missionaries arrived in Cambodia in 1990, they worked vigorously to create a national church. The relationship between missionaries and nationals has been a work in progress

---

[11]Saw Allen, Russell H. Bowers, Jr., and Dilani Senapatiratne, *Folk Buddhism in Southeast Asia*, 3.

[12]Joe Bruce, "The Critical Role of Relationships in Missions," *Evangelical Missions Quarterly* 47 (2011): 312.

ever since and has seen changes in relationships on both sides. The missionaries have gradually evolved from being parental providers to being brothers and sisters who walk alongside the pastors and leaders within the AGC. Although challenges have accompanied these changes, the overall relationship has been mutually positive, all the while seeing growth and advancement.

The years 1999-2008 serve as a reminder within the AG of the challenges that can arise due to lack of unity among both missionaries and nationals. While the subsequent years have seen advancement of ministry and partnership, more still must be done. It seems that, in most countries, the missionaries participate in their own retreats and fellowship to enjoy time together as one specific group. More recently, many of the AG missionaries in Cambodia who represent various countries have joined together annually for multiple days of worship and prayer. Such times to meet for fellowship can be understood as sharing life together as part of the AG in Cambodia. Little agenda is necessary aside from being reminded how fellowship and harmony can lead to more effective service for the glory of God.

The most productive times in the history of the AG in Cambodia have always coincided with unity between pastors and missionaries. This was exemplified in the 1990s as the national church was founded through partnership and made efforts to minister side by side in the most effective manner. Unfortunately, in the 2000s, differences in ministerial approaches led to a measure of distrust and division. However, 2014-2015 saw a return to unity due to national leaders welcoming missionaries to be more involved in AGC meetings and events.

Some have argued that gathering with different countries' missionaries and pastors could produce challenges due to the representation of multiple cultures and values, but a mutual understanding among a bicultural structure in ministry can certainly unite pastors and missionaries.[13] It is apparent that regular, open communication will preserve unity, because there will be recognition that God has strategically called people for a certain task and positioned them to serve together. A vital way this can be maintained is by missionaries and pastors meeting at the beginning of each year to discuss goals for that year, refer to key events in which both parties can join together in ministry and fellowship, and designate regular prayer times to encourage one another.

Leader Training

The past few decades in Cambodia have demonstrated openness to the gospel, in addition to a plethora of ways to resource Khmer believers. Areas such as prayer, stewardship, spiritual warfare, and worship have been continually addressed by cross-cultural workers from multiple countries. However, it is the area of training leaders via seminars, workshops, time-tested curricula, and new materials that have brought groups and individuals (who have not properly understood worldview or religion) to assist missionaries and nationals.[14] While often leader training has been connected to short-term meetings, the benefits have been minimal, because the training was arranged and delivered in haste.

Seminars, which are extremely popular in Christian circles in Cambodia, tend to be conducted over just a few days, which allow too little time to truly challenge believers in such an important area as leadership. Furthermore, while such training can provide temporary encouragement, it often fails to

---

[13]Paul G. Hiebert, *Anthropological Reflections on Missiological Issues*, (Grand Rapids, Michigan: Baker Books, 1994), 154.

[14]Craig Parro, "Asking Tough Questions: What Really Happens When We Train Leaders," *Evangelical Missions Quarterly* 48 (2011): 26.

adequately address important issues that could enrich the ministries of those individuals coming from outside Cambodia who don't have a clear understanding of the Khmer context. These factors have personified much of the Christian growth in Cambodia since the early 1990s. Seasoned Khmer pastors and veteran missionaries generally agree that there has been quick growth without the necessary depth necessary to provide long-term, positive results, such as believers having an abundant life, and churches progressing in their ministries. Thus, leaders are left in a position of not being fully equipped to lead as well as not understanding the fullness of their call to ministry.

There are also misconceptions that have been continually associated with leadership in Cambodia. Typically, Khmer leaders in the church are seen by the laity as that ultimate authority who possess the right to lord over others. They also are viewed as possessing remarkable character merely because of their position. The former aspect is generally due to the traditional patterns of leadership in the country, while the latter is based on positive assumptions of the laity. (However, domineering leadership has not been embraced by the younger generation, as the country continues to progress and become more modern.) The assumption that leaders automatically have remarkable character, however, is of greater concern because it deals directly with the spiritual well-being of pastor and church. It must be emphasized among the Khmer that being a church leader does not necessarily equate to an elevated standing, and those who try to minister without a foundation of genuine spirituality will not succeed.[15] Unfortunately, this persona is commonly demonstrated in Cambodia as leaders are seen as being superior in rank, far removed from others, and exempt from serving merely because of their position.

---

[15]Norman Shawchuck and Roger Heuser, *Leading the Congregation*, (Nashville, TN: Abingdon Press, 1993), 121.

Paul's epistles to Timothy and Titus demonstrate the nature of proper leadership in the church—leadership that focuses on character in addition to approach. Faithfulness and godliness are emphasized as Paul admonishes Timothy and Titus to see that future leaders are properly established. His primary emphasis relates to long-duration, practical, and encouraging means, which are only accomplished by investing, teaching, and imparting within the lives of future leaders. It is through these patterns that leadership must be understood, especially by those involved in cross-cultural ministry.

As missionaries in Cambodia endeavor to see that the next generation of leaders is adequately trained, they must remember the necessity at hand. Various methods, both in and out of the classroom, may be used; however, that training must be accomplished with the overall intention of strengthening the Body of Christ. Moreover, it must be connected to urgency, be related to God's calling, and look ahead to bountiful possibilities for those who will be developed.[16] The younger generation within Cambodia is longing for genuine leaders who serve with steadfast character and labor to see the Body of Christ enriched. Many of them have witnessed that, even if leaders demonstrate surpassing vision and fortitude, people will not follow them if there is a lack of God's purpose.[17] It is the responsibility of missionaries to ensure the necessary standards that will adequately train leaders who are genuinely called to serve the people of God in accordance with his will.

The AG in Cambodia has been enriched through the ministry of two Bible schools—Cambodia Bible Institute (CBI) and Cambodia School of Missions (CSM). Both schools have distinguished themselves in the fellowship through the training

---

[16]Greg Ogden, *Transforming Discipleship: Making Disciples a Few at a Time* (Downers Grove, IL: Inter Varsity Press, 2003), 38.

[17]Norman Shawchuck and Roger Heuser, *Leading the Congregation,* 148.

of pastors, leaders, and church planters among the Khmer. As the AGC continues to grow, there will be an even greater need for trained leaders to serve in various ministry capacities and impact the next generation in Cambodia. There have been missionaries and pastors who have debated the situation regarding Bible schools and declared that this type of ministry preparation should be replaced with other ways of training and mentoring. Some pastors believe schools and institutes that focus on training leaders can be disruptive to the overall plan of indigenous ministry and should concentrate on teaching at the grassroots level.

Many of those national pastors who do not endorse Bible schools feel training should be their prerogative for two reasons: (1) they already have a position of leadership to train according to their own preferences, and (2) they believe that potential leaders trained by others could undermine the pastors' position of authority in the local church. However, the patterns associated with Bible schools have been proven worldwide and they create an atmosphere for students to grow in their callings. To have designated institutions for training leaders allows individuals to focus specifically on their call to ministry, be in an environment with like-minded people, receive training from those specializing in applicable areas, and develop into their future roles as leaders. These are the key reasons CBI and CSM were started, and they serve as chief resources within the AGC to train leaders who are duly equipped to minister among the Khmer.

Discipleship Training

During the earliest years of the AG in Cambodia, missionaries used a variety of methods within numerous compassion ministries to maintain their presence and serve the Khmer. When church ministries developed as the national church was launched, discipleship was generally overlooked by pastors and leaders. Although growth occurred during the 1990s and 2000s, the challenges associated with a lack of discipleship became more evident because there was insufficient depth. By and large, this issue continues not only within the AG, but also in other denominations throughout Cambodia, since the pattern has been for missionaries to focus on quantity rather than quality.

Once again, seminars had dominated churches as a primary means of addressing the big problems. Those seminars often consisted of bringing in outside individuals who didn't understand Khmer cultural dynamics. Pastors and missionaries alike now acknowledge the roots that were planted in the early 1990s led to stunted growth and a lack of long-term fruit. Rather than focusing on the necessity of Christian education through Sunday schools and discipleship programs, leaders looked to the outside to resolve needs, rather than looking at ways to cultivate essential growth in believers.

Some may argue that the challenges related to discipleship stem from cultural issues. On the contrary, we can see God truly at work in culture and the power of the gospel penetrating and transforming regardless of culture.[18] The challenges related to discipleship are not cultural issues or problems, since successful models and approaches have been employed among people groups around the world. However, it's the foundation of culture followed by structure that ultimately brings progression.

Discipleship structures within Cambodian churches have tried a range of approaches, such as classroom settings, informal gatherings, and small groups, in order to provide enhanced accountability. And each of these approaches has resulted in a measure of growth and development in the lives of the believers.

---

[18]David J. Hesselgrave, *Communicating Christ Cross-Culturally* (Grand Rapids, MI: Zondervan Books, 1991), 128.

But once again, the issue is neither culture nor the overall structure; the problem lies in the process of implementation, which demonstrates a lack of resolved commitment and unwillingness to take the necessary time. Many national pastors and leaders are focusing on things they do not have rather than utilizing their own spiritual gifts and the abilities of others. For instance, one pastor lamented his need of books and teachers in order to have a successful discipleship program, instead of taking the time and effort to work with the mature Christians in his own church. When asked about their churches' discipleship programs (or lack of them), many pastors respond by saying their sermons are providing the instruction necessary to enable their members to grow spiritually. This reveals a serious misunderstanding of discipleship, in addition to neglect toward the Body of Christ in Cambodia at large.

In 2006, and again in 2010-11, veteran missionary Steve Hyde surveyed 644 Khmer pastors and church leaders in an effort to gauge the overall status of Christianity in Cambodia, especially regarding the area of discipleship. The survey findings seemed to underscore the crucial need for missionaries to develop ways by which Khmer believers can receive necessary attention as they are discipled. Key among those findings were these: 38% of respondents had regular teaching for new believers for the purpose of discipleship;[19] and 27% of respondents relied solely on weekly preaching for discipling new believers.[20]

A challenging and convicting word arises from this scenario—*process.* Regardless of setting, country, or people group, discipleship must be seen as a relationship that requires investing in people with the ultimate goal of transformation.[21]

---

[19]Steven John Hyde, "A Missiological and Critical Study of Cambodia's Historical, Cultural, and Sociopolitical Characteristics to Identify the Factors of Rapid Church Growth and Propose its Future Prognosis,"122.

[20]Ibid.

[21]Greg Ogden, *Transforming Discipleship,* 17.

The lack of opportunities, such as relying only on sermons, or forgoing altogether a discipleship class, has failed to make an impact on believers. This is shown even among beginning Bible school students, most of whom are deficient in basic Bible knowledge and are unable to share fundamental doctrines with others.

In Cambodia, discipleship should not be considered as just another program for the sake of mere continuance in the church, but must be part of each group and emulated in daily life. Missionaries need to be directly involved and take the initiative to consider discipleship as a major ministry within churches, as it will not only transform lives, but also shape the future of Christianity in Cambodia. One example is the Christian Life Program (CLP), a discipleship effort launched by AG missionaries in 2011 to address these concerns and provide opportunities for AGC church members to grow in their faith. Consisting of courses on Bible study methods, life in Christ, basic Christian doctrine, and sharing the gospel, the program has been taught by experienced pastors and missionaries at multiple sites across the country. Adding this program to valued relationships can be vital for multiplication and transformation through progressive fellowship. [22]

Insights for the Assemblies of God Cambodia (AGC)

Goals

Since its official recognition in 1997, the AGC proved itself to be a significant fellowship in Cambodia, launched numerous churches and ministries, experienced internal changes, and encountered challenges. Many of its earliest pastors and leaders lived through the tragedies of civil war, genocide, and

----

[22]Ibid.

Vietnamese occupation to later find Christ and receive a call to minister. Their early years of ministry came at the most fitting time, as the Khmer were in the process of rebuilding all aspects of life and culture. The overall significance of the AGC is remarkable considering Christianity's recovery from near-extinction in Cambodia.

The AGC has experienced seasons of growth during times of resourcing the fellowship through ministries in cities and rural areas. However, it has also experienced seasons of simply maintaining the status quo in which churches struggled due to a lack of connectivity within the overall structure. It appears that ebb and flow, which has been repeated, can be prevented by continually reaffirming vital goals with regard to existence and ministry. Although the AGC can still be considered first generation, the leadership is now in the second generation and must be ready to take the fellowship to a higher level.[23] The question, "What are our goals?" must be repeatedly asked by both leaders and laity if the AGC expects to strive forward into the future.

An examination of the first centuries within Christianity demonstrates basic principles that enabled the Church to clearly understand its intentions and functions as the Body of Christ. Three key aspects are noticeably distinct as the early Church flourished in spite of persecution and cultural shifts. The areas of canon, episcopacy, and creed not only stabilized the church in the midst of challenging times, but also facilitated the necessary structure for the succeeding centuries.[24] A basic approach with this in mind can provide the necessary framework to lead the AGC, provide its intentions, and describe its functions in ministry.

---

[23]Clements, interview by author.

[24]Mark A. Noll, *Turning Points: Decisive Moments in the History of Christianity* (Grand Rapids, MI: Baker Academic, 2012), 25.

Three things are necessary for the Assemblies of God Cambodia to thrive. First, the Word of God must be maintained as the authoritative rule of faith and conduct. Numerous cults have appeared in Cambodia over the past decades. Too many churches have become susceptible to false doctrine because they failed to prioritize the Bible as the ultimate standard. Ministering the Word of God is to always be the primary goal within the fellowship. Second, the role of church leaders must be clearly understood according to one's calling, implemented with the highest regard, and held accountable by the national church. The system of leadership in the early Church serves as an example in these three areas, as it oversaw internal issues and coordinated ministry efforts to evangelize the lost.[25] Third, creeds and statements of faith must be embraced to provide what a church believes and practices. The AGC is in a strategic position as the leading Pentecostal denomination in Cambodia, and its leadership should repeatedly emphasize this uniqueness related to the fellowship's intentions and functions.

Clarity in Church Structure

Accountability issues have brought frequent challenges within the AGC's history. Areas inside and outside the church, including ministry, finances, and morality, have been called into question, with some groups of believers left in shame and disrepute. The question, "How should clarity be maintained?" must be addressed if the AGC is to model the Biblical patterns of the Body of Christ as found in 1 Corinthians 12 and Ephesians 4. One example that can be found in the early history of the AG in Cambodia is represented by the first church to be recognized in the fellowship—Jerusalem Church.

---

[25]Ibid., 32.

There is a story about a missionary who visited Jerusalem Church in the early 1990s to view its ministries and meet with the leadership. The missionary was quite impressed with the church's structure and remarked about its overall continuity. The church leaders explained how their three-tiered system of leadership provided necessary clarity and enabled the church to avoid problems.[26] This particular structure, comprised of the pastoral team, the elders, and a ministry committee, proved more than adequate to handle all church matters and effectively minister to the needs of the church.

This pattern provides three ways that support church effectiveness. First, this composition of leadership allowed the pastoral team to provide vision and properly serve as shepherds. Jerusalem Church had two lead pastors, with both responsible for preaching and both sharing the internal and external duties; thus, one pastor could manage any in-house situations while the other could focus on ministry needs outside the church. Second, the elders maintained accountability within the overall leadership structure and provided perspective when any issues arose. Third, the ministry committee provided stability and was responsible for the initiation of programs. This structure allowed the church to be active in discipleship within the church and to provide evangelism outside the church.

Such a three-tiered system of leadership could work within other AGC churches, since it supplies strength internally and externally, maintains accountability on all levels, balances the levels of leadership, and provides the all-important facet of clarity. This structural model would prevent domineering leaders from having complete control over the church and allow alignment with Biblical patterns of church structure so as to facilitate effective ministry.

---

[26]Heng, interview by author.

Outward Focus

The years of rebuilding that followed the genocide and Vietnamese occupation caused the entire country to be dependent upon assistance in order for infrastructure to be properly situated. Cambodia was still full of chaos and change as 22,000 United Nations soldiers arrived, billions of dollars poured into the country, countless thousands remained in refugee camps, and the Khmer Rouge continued to raid the innocent.[27] Christianity was also dependent on outside sources to assist in the recovery process, as there were only about 200 Christians and few leaders by the year 1989. Internal structure progressed slowly as missions' groups and parachurch organizations assisted the weary, war-torn Khmer believers.

Denominations and fellowships were blessed by the giving of others throughout the rebuilding and stabilizing of Christianity in the 1990s. Those Khmer believers associated with the AG were also recipients during those particular years to generate a national church and plan for productive ministries in the future. Today, the AGC is in a position of self-governance, since missionaries serve in a partnering, rather than a providing role. There now is definite strength as the pastors and churches are realizing their potential, yet more can be done as the AGC moves forward to minister. The question, "What is an appropriate focus to attain goals?" must be asked as future ministry is strategized.

Since the AGC has been continually making necessary changes such as revisions to its constitution, updates to levels of credentialing, and the structuring of districts to enhance the internal framework, now is the time for a greater external focus. Capable leaders and solid practitioners have been produced from within Cambodia and have demonstrated effective

[27]Don Cormack, *Killing Fields, Living Fields,* 401.

ministry. Now, the AGC has reached a stage of utilizing its assets and is becoming primed to concentrate more on outward evangelism. Some churches have caught this vision as they single-handedly minister through youth events, children's outreaches, and health clinics. However, these are exceptions rather than the norm.

The AGC is in a position to do more than ever before as it adjusts its methods to become increasingly stronger with an outward focus. The days of complete dependence and growing pains have been endured, with valuable lessons learned throughout those processes. Evangelism is the next crucial step, allowing the AGC to expand even more ministries, that will not only impact the Khmer, but also have the potential to cross borders. This particular approach has proven successful in various Asian settings, as aggressive outreach and creative evangelism have become an impetus for other ministries.[28] AGC pastors and church leaders have been discussing the possibilities of sending missionaries and missions teams abroad on a regular basis. For this to properly occur, local evangelism coming from churches must be a focal point, as this will be the appropriate predecessor before missions' ministries outside Cambodia can become fully implemented.

Holistic and Pentecostal

Ministry in Cambodia is approached in countless ways, many times with new trends being embraced then later discarded, only to search again for a suitable replacement. The AGC has experienced these cycles due to the popularity of seminars and conferences with "outsiders" discussing popular

---

[28]Saphir P. Athyal, "Toward an Asian Christian Theology," in *The Bible and Theology in Asian Contexts*, ed. Bong Rin Ro and Ruth Eshenaur, (Seoul, South Korea: Word of Life Press, 1991), 56.

ideologies that have been successful in non-Asian settings. The key question, "How should ministry be approached among our own?" can lead to a fundamental understanding of effective ways to minister among the Khmer. Two necessary approaches in Cambodia include being holistic and being Pentecostal.

Holistic models have made a significant impact among people groups throughout Asia, due to methods that focus on ministering the gospel through evangelism while addressing social needs.[29] This should be noted as an integral approach in Cambodia, since prior AG ministries were made to meet the heartfelt needs of the Khmer. The AGC served rural needs through its Community Health Evangelism (CHE) programs in 1999, which eventually developed into Cambodia Global Action (CGA). The programs within CGA have been generally separated from the ministry within the AGC, due to the distinction that had been made between spiritual concerns and social concerns. However, there is definite value when the two areas are combined in word and deed to proclaim the gospel and address the most basic needs. A combined effort that links these aspects through a holistic approach has the capability of transforming individuals, societies, and nations at every strata of life.[30] Both evangelistic efforts and rural programs are needed in the overall approach and can be maximized by having the AGC oversee the CGA to adequately minister spiritually and socially among the Khmer.

The AG in Cambodia has a unique opportunity to approach ministry not only through holistic efforts, but also through its Pentecostal distinction. The moving of the Holy Spirit in Cambodia was evident over the past 25 years, as Christianity has grown from mere hundreds of believers to hundreds of

---

[29]Samuel Jayakumar, "The Work of God as Holistic Mission: An Asian Perspective," *Evangelical Review of Theology* 35 (2011): 241.

[30]JoAnn Butrin, *From the Roots Up: A Closer Look at Compassion and Justice in Missions*, (Springfield, MO: Roots Up Publishers, 2010), 13.

thousands. In regard to the activity of the Spirit in a global sense, the overall impact continues to shape affections, intellect, and morality as it brings change both individually and socially.[31] AGC pastors and leaders must take note of these global patterns in order to fully recognize how God is working through the Spirit's activity. Understanding the full experience of being Pentecostal in addition to how it relates to ministerial approaches, will allow pastors and churches to see the impact both personally and culturally.[32]

One final way in which the AG in Cambodia can demonstrate its uniqueness through a combined holistic and Pentecostal approach should include the areas of signs, wonders, and miracles. Like many other places throughout Asia, the Khmer people in Cambodia are extremely superstitious and fervently connected to the spirit world. This type of worldview is characterized by continually explaining events based on spirit activity, with individuals seeking peace by trying to appease spirits.[33] Demonstration of the Holy Spirit's power is the primary catalyst for believers to authenticate God's authority over all other spirits. Signs, wonders, and miracles in Cambodia have proven to be efficacious when Khmer believers share the gospel not only in words, but also through the surpassing power that comes from the Holy Spirit.

Maintaining Kingdom Perspectives in Cambodia

Although Christianity has been in Cambodia for over 450 years, the recent decades have been the most critical. Near extinction caused the church to gradually discover its own

---

[31]Amos Yong, *The Spirit Poured Out on All Flesh* (Grand Rapids, MI: Baker Academic, 2005), 293.

[32]David Martin, *Pentecostalism: The World Their Parish* (Oxford, UK: Blackwell Publishers, Ltd., 2002), 167.

[33]Charles H. Kraft, *Christianity with Power,* 88.

identity through the process of comprehending its strengths and weaknesses.[34] By maintaining perspectives directly related to the kingdom of God, which can be seen as his supreme reign over creation and his salvific interaction with humankind, pastors and churches will have a greater clarity in their identity. This will allow them to be closely aligned with God's purposes and be able to increase their effectiveness in ministry.

For missionaries and pastors serving in Cambodia, it is imperative to maintain a kingdom perspective together and to recognize the crucial times and seasons. This perspective can be viewed through the aspects of past, present, and future as it demonstrates how the Lord has been building his church in Cambodia. Khmer believers are participating in the kingdom with full partnership, and the days to come can be met by resolve to strive forward. Perspectives affirmed in this manner display a willingness to serve in the Lord's work together with mutual collaboration among fellow believers. This will ultimately show the inherent value of the church and its purpose as being the primary agent of evangelism in the world.

Kingdom principles put into motion by missionaries and pastors in Cambodia will prioritize all aspects of ministry and have a definite impact on those who are served. It will be at this point that the value of the church will be expressed as the means used by God to minister to the lost, needy, and broken. This shows how the ministerial activity of missionaries and pastors is of utmost importance, since it conveys the message of Christ and displays a witness of the kingdom of God among nations and people groups.[35] Moreover, contemplating that kingdom through ministerial efforts will allow the missionaries and pastors to fulfill God's plans, rather than remain in a realm of

---

[34]Don Cormack, *Killing Fields, Living Fields*. 440.

[35]Howard A. Snyder, "The Church in God's Plan," in *Perspectives on the World Christian Movement 4ᵗʰ Edition*, ed. Ralph D. Winter and Steven Hawthorne (Pasadena, CA: William Carey Library, 2009), 155.

self-centered focus. As efforts are made to heed Christ's words and to seek the kingdom of God, an eternal focus will be firmly in place as well as reveal the fullness of God's presence to others.[36] Striving to embrace these principles in Cambodia can allow Christians to be firmly situated in God's will and serve in ways that bring glory to him.

Missionaries and pastors serving in Cambodia are recognizing their responsibility to stand firm, to convey the message of the kingdom of God, and to complete their task regardless of the challenges and opposition.[37] Khmer Christians have faced extreme hostility, not only from war, genocide, and political shifts, but also from direct the attacks of Satan himself. For centuries, the enemy has maintained dominion over much of Southeast Asia, and the strongholds that still exist throughout Cambodia demonstrate his intent to continue possessing this area. There is a definite spiritual war raging as two separate powers vie for control over the same territory.[38]

Churches in Cambodia have the tendency to limit their outward perception of God's reign and interaction with people due to looking at personal surroundings. A proper kingdom perspective would create a global outlook—one that eliminates narrow-sighted problems and frees pastors and congregations to minister in ways that are culturally relevant and biblically consistent.[39] This should be a primary goal of each church, as believers strive to keep the kingdom of God in full view and as

---

[36]Larry L. Niemeyer, *Cultural Anthropology,* 30.

[37]George Eldon Ladd, "The Gospel of the Kingdom," in *Perspectives on the World Christian Movement 4th Edition,* ed. Ralph D. Winter and Steven Hawthorne (Pasadena, CA: William Carey Library, 2009), 94.

[38]C. Peter Wagner, "On the Cutting Edge of Mission Strategy," in *Perspectives on the World Christian Movement 4th Edition,* ed. Ralph D. Winter and Steven Hawthorne (Pasadena, CA: William Carey Library, 2009), 581.

[39]Murray W. Dempster, "Evangelism, Social Concern, and the Kingdom of God," in *Called and Empowered: Global Mission in Pentecostal Perspective,* ed. Murray W. Dempster, Byron D. Klaus, and Douglas Petersen (Peabody, MA: Hendrickson Publishers, 1991), 33.

they serve among the Khmer. The leaders and laity alike can make it a priority to live and declare kingdom principles through their actions.

Whether via church ministries or social programs, the endeavors of the people of God are to be directly linked to his work among humanity. This speaks of how kingdom perspectives, when taken to heart, will cause the activity of the Body of Christ to display the reconciliatory love of Christ among nations, cultures, and people groups.[40] As this is wholeheartedly put into action, God's glory and blessing will be manifested in Cambodia and will not be limited by any barriers related to language, culture, or geography.

Cambodia has been viewed by many as a country without hope due to the tragic events of the past. However, the true nature of the church exhibits hope in the coming kingdom and is exemplified by its role to declare the message of the kingdom of God.[41] If these perspectives are taught by missionaries and pastors, in addition to being maintained by churches, Cambodia will witness the glory and blessing of God.

---

[40]Howard A. Snyder, "The Church in God's Plan," 155.

[41]Hesselgrave and Rommen, *Contextualization,* 43.

Final Thoughts

PSALM 126
(Song of ascents)
[1] When the LORD restored the fortunes of Zion,
we were like those who dreamed.
[2] Our mouths were filled with laughter,
our tongues with songs of joy.
Then it was said among the nations,
"The LORD has done great things for them."
[3] The LORD has done great things for us,
and we are filled with joy.
[4] Restore our fortunes, LORD,
like streams in the Negev.
[5] Those who sow with tears
will reap with songs of joy.
[6] Those who go out weeping,
carrying seed to sow,
will return with songs of joy,
carrying sheaves with them.

Psalm 126 speaks of the restoration of a people who return to their homeland, following seasons of hardship and tragedy. The notion of coming back to a familiar location invoked true joy and celebration by those who had dreamed of liberty and peace. As it comes to its conclusion, the psalm fittingly speaks of reaping. It alludes to this culmination as the people advance forward, with the most difficult days now behind them.

Although this particular psalm was written as a worship song for the Israelite exiles returning from captivity, there are similarities in regard to the Christians in Cambodia. Just as within the lives of God's chosen people in the Old Testament, the first verses speak from a historical point of view in noting the challenges and triumphs. And just as the final verses look ahead with Israel longing to be restored to their past greatness, so also the Christians in Cambodia are to look ahead with hope for God to provide a bountiful harvest among the Khmer.

The history of Christianity in Cambodia demonstrates countless challenges of the gospel being slowly planted among the Khmer. More than four centuries of initial missions' work produced very little, aside from persecutions and martyrdom, as Buddhism continually dominated the religious landscape. New opportunities in the 1920s led to 50 years of effective ministry by missionaries and pastors only to be overtaken by the horrors of war and genocide. However, God was always working in Cambodia, graciously saving a remnant and opening doors once again in 1990. Despite the times of sorrow and weeping throughout this harrowing history, the people of God have seen great things in their midst.

Reoccurring precedents within leadership plus cultural nuances have situated the Khmer in a unique place, as Buddhism's overarching presence has allowed for an identity that overshadowed the people and dictated their personal volition. Countless hardships and predicaments that the Khmer endured as a people group have generated never-ending questions with few viable answers. Their history and societal tendencies serve as a reminder for missionaries to understand the necessary components within culture that can ultimately determine ministerial advancements or shortcomings in the years to come.

Although certainly a very short timeframe, the years 1990-2015 show promise in regard to the events that have transpired, the effectiveness of present undertakings, and the unlimited potential for the future. Patterns and trends within those momentous years for the Assemblies of God can enable discernment, as the Fellowship learns from successes and failures. Many missionaries and pastors have lived out the story of mission and ministry among a broken people desperate to find the message of hope in Christ. Timing has been crucial as the AG has grown in Cambodia and will continue to be significant for the Fellowship to remain a catalyst within the next generation.

It is fitting that the first 25 years of the AG in Cambodia would conclude with a credentialing service on December 1, 2015. Among those gathered to watch the ceremony in the chapel at Cambodia Bible Institute were men and women who had survived the genocide in the 1970s, suffered through displacement and rebuilding in the 1980s, and surrendered to Christ in the 1990s. All had made numerous sacrifices, as they gave their lives to participate in reaping among the Khmer. Standing before them was a group of 20 individuals called by God, proven in ministry, and ready to enter the harvest fields. As these 14 men and six women knelt to be prayed over by missionaries and pastors, there was great realization about the opportune beginnings, continual progression, and enduring optimism for the future in Cambodia.

Bibliography

Allen, Saw, Russell H. Bowers, Jr., and Dilani Senapatiratne. *Folk Buddhism in Southeast Asia*. Phnom Penh, Cambodia: Training of Timothys, 2003.

Ath, The. Interview by author. August 4, 2016.

Athyal, Saphir P. "Toward an Asian Christian Theology." In *The Bible and Theology in Asian Contexts*, ed. Bong Rio Ro and Ruth Eshenaur. Seoul, South Korea: Word of Life Press, 1991.

Bit, Seanglim. *The Warrior Heritage: A Psychological Perspective of Cambodian Trauma*. El Cerrito, CA: Seanglim Bit, 1991.

Bruce, Joe W. "The Critical Role of Relationships in Missions." In *Evangelical Missions Quarterly Vol. 47*, ed. A. Scott Moreau. Wheaton, IL: Wheaton College, 2011.

Burnett, David. *The Spirit of Buddhism*. London, UK: Monarch Books, 1996.

Butrin, JoAnn. *From the Roots Up: A Closer Look at Compassion and Justice in Missions*. Springfield, MO: Roots Up Publishers, 2010.

Cambodian Christian.com. Church History—Chronology of the Cambodian Christian Church. http://www.cambodianchristian.com/church_history_p5.htm on September 12, 2016 (accessed September 12, 2016).

Chandler, David P. *A History of Cambodia*, 2nd ed. Chiang Mai, Thailand: Silkworm Books, 1998.

Chandler, David P. *The Land and People of Cambodia*. New York, NY: Harper Collins Publishers, 1991.

Chandler, David P. *The Tragedy of Cambodian History*. Chiang Mai, Thailand: Silkworm Books, 1993.

Clements, Darin and Dianna Clements. Interview by author. August 23, 2016.

Clements, Darin and Ken Huff. "The Pentecostal Movement in Cambodia"(Paper presented for the Assemblies of God Missionary Fellowship, July 2015).

Cormack, Don. *Killing Fields, Living Fields*. London, UK: Monarch Books, 2001.

De Castro, Joaquim Magalhães. "Great Figures of the Missionary Work." http://www.oclarim.com.mo/ en/2016/07/01/gaspar-da-cruz-the-dominican-traveller-5/ (accessed August 18, 2016).

DeFalco, Randle C. "Justice and Starvation in Cambodia: The Khmer Rouge Famine." In *The Cambodian Law and Policy Journal Iss. 2*, ed. Anne Heindel. Phnom Penh, Cambodia: Documentation Center of Cambodia, 2014.

Dempster, Murray W. "Evangelism, Social Concern, and the Kingdom of God." In *Called and Empowered: Global Mission in Pentecostal Perspective*, ed. Murray W. Dempster, Byron D. Klaus, and Douglas Petersen. Peabody, MA: Hendrickson Publishers, 1991.

Dorsey, Carolyn. "History of ICA Phnom Penh," (Paper presented for the Assemblies of God Missionary Fellowship, 2000).

Dorsey, Carolyn. "Information Regarding the Founding of the Assemblies of God Work in Cambodia," (Paper presented for the Assemblies of God Missionary Fellowship, 2005).

Encyclopedia.com. The Catholic Church in Cambodia. http://www.encyclopedia.com/article-1G2-3407701938/cambodia-catholic-church.html (accessed August 18, 2016).

Eng, Sam Ath. Interview by author. August 10, 2016.

Gottesman, Evan. *Cambodia After the Khmer Rouge.* New Haven, CT: Yale University Press, 2003.

Greve, Ann. Interview by author. August 31, 2016.

Heawood, Edward. *A History of Geographical Discovery in the Seventeenth and Eighteenth Centuries.* New York, NY: Cambridge University Press, 2012.

Heng, Cheng. Interview by author. August 15, 2016.

Hesselgrave, David J. *Communicating Christ Cross-Culturally.* Grand Rapids, MI: Zondervan Books, 1991.

Hesselgrave, David J. and Edward Rommen *Contextualization: Meanings, Methods and Models* Pasadena, CA: William Carey Library, 1989.

Hiebert, Paul G. *Anthropological Insights for Missionaries.* Grand Rapids, MI: Baker Books, 1985.

Hiebert, Paul G. *Anthropological Reflections on Missiological Issues.* Grand Rapids, MI: Baker Books, 1994.

Huff, Ken. Interview by author. August 8, 2016.

Hyde, Steven John. "A Missiological and Critical Study of Cambodia's Historical, Cultural, and Sociopolitical Characteristics to Identify the Factors of Rapid Church Growth and Propose its Future Prognosis." PhD diss., Bethany International University, 2015.

International Christian Assembly Cambodia. http://www.ica-cambodia.org/ (accessed August 21, 2016).

Jayakumar, Samuel. "The Work of God as Holistic Mission: An Asian Perspective." In *Evangelical Review of Theology Vol. 35*, ed. David Parker. Broadstairs, Kent, UK: King's Evangelical Divinity School, 2011.

Joshua Project. Cambodia. https://joshuaproject.net/
     countries/CB (accessed October 15, 2016).

Kraft, Charles H. *Anthropology for Christian Witness.*
     Maryknoll, NY: Orbis Books, 1996.

Kraft, Charles H. *Christianity with Power.* Grand Rapids, MI:
     Servant Books, 1989.

Kraft, Charles H. "Culture, Worldview, and Contextualization."
     In *Perspectives on the World Christian Movement 4th*
     Edition, ed. Ralph D. Winter and Steven Hawthorne.
     Pasadena, CA: William Carey Library. 2009.

Kraft, Marguerite G. *Understanding Spiritual Power: A*
     Forgotten Dimension of Cross-Cultural Mission and
     Ministry. Maryknoll, NY: Orbis Books, 1995.

Ladd, George Eldon. "The Gospel of the Kingdom." In
     Perspectives on the World Christian Movement 4th
     Edition, ed. Ralph D. Winter and Steven Hawthorne.
     Pasadena, CA: William Carey Library, 2009.

Lingenfelter, Sherwood G., and Marvin K Mayers. *Ministering*
     Cross-Culturally: An Incarnational Model for Personal
     Relationships. Grand Rapids, MI: Baker Books, 1986.

Maddux, Ron. "The Assemblies of God in Cambodia,"
     (Sermon at International Christian Assembly, Phnom Penh,
     Cambodia, January 27, 2016).

Maher, Brian with Uon Seila. *Cry of the Gecko.* Centralia,
     WA: Gorham Printing, 2012.

Martin, David. *Pentecostalism: The World Their Parish.*
     Oxford, UK: Blackwell Publishers, Ltd., 2002.

Moffett, Samuel Hugh. *A History of Christianity in Asia Vol.*
     II: 1500-1900. Maryknoll, NY: Orbis Books, 2005.

Neill, Stephen. *A History of Christian Missions*, 2nd ed.
     Revised. London, UK: Penguin Books, 1991.

Niemeyer, Larry L. *Cultural Anthropology: Cultural Studies for Ministry Practitioners: Readings and Resource Materials.* Springfield, MO: Global University, 2006.

Noll, Mark A. *Turning Points: Decisive Moments in the History of Christianity,* 3rd ed. Grand Rapids, MI: Baker Academic, 2012.

Ogden, Greg. *Transforming Discipleship: Making Disciples a Few at a Time.* Downers Grove, IL: Inter Varsity Press, 2003.

Parro, Craig. "Asking Tough Questions: What Really Happens When We Train Leaders?" *Evangelical Missions Quarterly* (January 2012). https://www.emqonline.com/node/2634 (accessed September 13, 2016).

Robinette, Kelly. Interview by author. August 1, 2016.

Saiyasak, Chansamone. "Southeast Asia Christianity." https://www.academia.edu/4781739/Southeast_Asia_Christianity (accessed August 12, 2016).

Shaw, R. Daniel and Charles E. Van Engen. *Communicating God's Word in a Complex World: God's Truth or Hocus Pocus?* Oxford, UK: Rowman and Littlefield Publishers, Inc., 2003.

Shawchuck, Norman and Roger Heuser. *Leading the Congregation.* Nashville, TN: Abingdon Press, 1993.

Snyder, Howard A. "The Church in God's Plan." In *Perspectives on the World Christian Movement 4th Edition,* ed. Ralph D. Winter and Steven Hawthorne. Pasadena, CA: William Carey Library, 2009.

Tino, James. "A Lesson from Jose: Understanding the Patron/Client Relationship." In *Evangelical Missions Quarterly.* https://missionexus.org/a-lesson-from-jose-understanding-the-patron-client-relationship/ (accessed August 28, 2016).

Van Rheenen, Gailyn. "A Theology of Power." *Evangelical Missions Quarterly* (January 2005). http://www.emqonline.com/node/339 (accessed September 13, 2016).

Wagner, C. Peter. "On the Cutting Edge of Mission Strategy." In *Perspectives on the World Christian Movement 4th Edition*, ed. Ralph D. Winter and Steven Hawthorne. Pasadena, CA: William Carey Library, 2009.

Weerasingha, Tissa. "Karma and Christ: Opening Our Eyes to the Buddhist World." In *International Journal of Frontier Missions Vol.* 10, ed. Hans M. Weerstra. El Paso, TX: International Student Leaders Coalition for Frontier Missions, 1993.

Yong, Amos. *The Spirit Poured Out on All Flesh: Pentecostalism and the Possibility of Global Theology*. Grand Rapids, MI: Baker Academic, 2005.

Appendices

Timeline of Christianity in Cambodia

1555
Gaspar da Cruz becomes the first missionary to serve in
Cambodia.

1636
Dutch Christians become the first Protestant missionaries in
Cambodia.

1863
There are approximately 600 Christians in Cambodia.

1923
Arthur Hammond and David Ellison arrive with their families
to serve as missionaries with the Christian and Missionary
Alliance (CMA). The Hammonds begin to translate the Bible
in Phnom Penh and the Ellisons start a Bible school in
Battambang.

1933

Arthur Hammond completes his translation of the New Testament.

1953

Arthur Hammond and the CMA complete the translation of the Bible.

1965

- The Cambodian government forces American Protestant missionaries to leave the country.

- There are approximately 1,000 Christians in Cambodia.

1970

- Foreign missionaries are allowed to return to Cambodia.

- There are approximately 7,500 Christians in Cambodia, most of whom are Catholic.

1975

There are approximately 10,000 Christians in Cambodia.

1975-1979

Approximately 2,000,000 Khmer, including the vast majority of Christians, are killed by the Khmer Rouge through execution, starvation, and disease.

1979

There are approximately 150 Christians in Cambodia following the genocide.

1989

There are approximately 200 Christians in Cambodia.

1990

The Cambodian government formally recognizes Christianity yet proselytizing is forbidden.

1993

National elections are held in Cambodia and allow more freedom for Christians.

1996

The Evangelical Fellowship of Cambodia (EFC) is created.

1997

- Today's Khmer Version of the Bible is published.
- A political coup forces missionaries to leave the country for a short time.
- There are approximately 500 churches and 20,000 Christians in Cambodia.

2005

Today's Khmer Version of the Bible is edited. And the name is changed to the Khmer Standard Version.

2015

There are approximately 250,000 Christians in Cambodia.

APPENDIX B

Timeline of the Assemblies of God in Cambodia

1990
- Bob Houlihan and Ron Maddux are the first AG ministers to arrive in Cambodia.
- Randy and Carolyn Dorsey become the first appointed AG missionaries to reside in Cambodia.
- International Christian Assembly (ICA) holds its first services.
- Jerusalem Church becomes associated with the AG.

1991
- An English center is founded in Phnom Penh.
- Medical clinics are started in the provinces.

1992
- Hospitals, orphanages, and schools are established in the provinces.
- Jerusalem Church is officially recognized as first AG church in Cambodia.

1993
The first class of Cambodia Bible Institute (CBI) is held.

1994
- CBI is officially chartered with the government.
- Heng Cheng and Andrew Kuong become the first credentialed AG ministers in Cambodia.
- The first formal AG pastors' meetings are held in Phnom Penh.

1996

The AG becomes part of the Evangelical Fellowship Cambodia (EFC).

1997

- The Assemblies of God Cambodia (AGC) is officially recognized by the government.
- The AGC has its first elections and adopts a formal constitution.

1999

- Community Health Evangelism (CHE) programs begin.
- The AGC's constitution is revised.

2000

Twelve pastors are officially recognized and credentialed by the AGC.

2002

Various programs and projects are handed over to the government.

2004

Cambodia Global Action (CGA) is established as a Non-Government Organization (NGO).

2006

Seventeen pastors are officially recognized and credentialed by the AGC.

2007

Five pastors are officially recognized and credentialed by the AGC.

2008

- The AG breaks ground for new buildings on the CBI campus. The project is conducted to provide offices and classrooms for CBI, ICA, AGC, and Assemblies of God Missionary Fellowship (AGMF).
- Three pastors are officially recognized and credentialed by the AGC.

2009

- Cambodia School of Missions (CSM) is established.
- Eleven pastors are officially recognized and credentialed by the AGC.

2010

The AGC creates six geographical districts within its fellowship.

2011

- The building project on the CBI campus is completed with new offices and classrooms.
- The Christian Life Program for discipleship begins in Siem Reap.

2015

Twenty pastors are officially recognized and credentialed by the AGC.

www.ingramcontent.com/pod-product-compliance
Lightning Source LLC
Chambersburg PA
CBHW071103090426
42737CB00013B/2450